TAKE A STEP TO STAMP OUT TORTURE

Amnesty International

- **Take a step to stamp out torture** — join Amnesty International's campaign against torture
- Join Amnesty International and other local and international human rights organizations which fight torture
- Make a donation to support Amnesty International's work
- Tell friends and family about the campaign and ask them to join too
- Register to take action against torture at **www.stoptorture.org** and campaign online. Visitors to the website will be able to appeal on behalf of individuals at risk of torture

Cover: Ethnic Albanian refugees from Kosovo in the Stenkovec 1 refugee camp in Macedonia. Some 850,000 ethnic Albanians fled or were forcibly expelled from Kosovo between March and June 1999. They were fleeing gross human rights violations including "disappearances", torture and killings.
© Kent Klich/Magnum Photos

Amnesty International (AI) is a worldwide movement of people who campaign for human rights. AI works towards the observance of all human rights as enshrined in the Universal Declaration of Human Rights and other international standards. It seeks to promote the observance of the full range of human rights, which it considers to be indivisible and interdependent, through campaigning and public awareness activities, as well as through human rights education and pushing for ratification and implementation of human rights treaties.

AI's work is based on careful research and on the standards agreed by the international community. AI is a voluntary, democratic, self-governing movement with more than a million members and supporters in more than 140 countries and territories. It is funded largely by its worldwide membership and by donations from the public. No funds are sought or accepted from governments for AI's work in documenting and campaigning against human rights violations.

AI is independent of any government, political persuasion or religious creed. It does not support or oppose any government or political system, nor does it support or oppose the views of the victims whose rights it seeks to protect. It is concerned solely with the impartial protection of human rights.

AI takes action against some of the gravest violations by governments of people's civil and political rights. The focus of its campaigning against human rights violations is to:

- free all prisoners of conscience. According to AI's statute, these are people detained for their political, religious or other conscientiously held beliefs or because of their ethnic origin, sex, colour, language, national or social origin, economic status, birth or other status – who have not used or advocated violence;
- ensure fair and prompt trials for all political prisoners;
- abolish the death penalty, torture and ill-treatment;
- end political killings and "disappearances".

AI calls on armed political groups to respect human rights and to halt abuses such as the detention of prisoners of conscience, hostage-taking, torture and unlawful killings.

AI also seeks to support the protection of human rights by other activities, including its work with the United Nations (UN) and regional intergovernmental organizations, and its work for refugees, on international military, security and police relations, and on economic and cultural relations.

TAKE A STEP TO STAMP OUT TORTURE

Amnesty International Publications

Please note that some of the photographs and case histories contained in this report may be disturbing.

First published in 2000 by
Amnesty International Publications
1 Easton Street
London WC1X 0DW
United Kingdom

www.amnesty.org

© Copyright
Amnesty International Publications 2000
ISBN: 0 86210 292 8
AI Index: ACT 40/13/00
Original language: English

Designed by: Synergy

Printed by:
The Alden Press
Osney Mead
Oxford
United Kingdom

All rights reserved. No part of this publication may be reproduced, stored in a retrieval system, or transmitted, in any form or by any means, electronic, mechanical, photocopying, recording and/or otherwise without the prior permission of the publishers.

TAKE A STEP TO STAMP OUT TORTURE

Contents

Introduction 1

Chapter 1: Torture today 9
    Torture at the hands of the police 16
    Cruel, inhuman or degrading
    conditions of detention 21
    "Lawful torture": judicial corporal punishment 24
    Violence in the home and community 28
    Torture — a weapon of war 32

Chapter 2: Discrimination: fertile ground for torture 37
    Racism and torture 39
    Torture of women 46
    Torture and sexual identity 54
    Torture of children 62

Chapter 3: Impunity 69
    Impunity — a worldwide problem 70
    Obstacles to justice 73
    No safe haven for torturers 81
    International tribunals 83

Chapter 4: Fighting torture: an agenda for action 87
    Preventing torture: safeguards in custody 91
    Strategy-building 95
    Using the international system against torture 97
    The battle for hearts and minds 100
    Stopping the torture trade 102
    Protecting people fleeing from torture 107
    Medical professionals and torture 110
    Treatment of torture survivors 112
    Recommendations 115

What you can do 122

Appendix 1:
    AI's 12-Point Program for the Prevention of
    Torture by Agents of the State 124

Appendix 2:
    International standards against torture (extracts) 128

Appendix 3:
    UN Convention against Torture, ratifications,
    declarations and reservations 131

Endnotes 136

In this report, the abbreviation UN Convention against Torture has been used to refer to the UN Convention against Torture and Other Cruel, Inhuman or Degrading Treatment or Punishment. Similarly the UN Declaration on the Protection of All Persons from Being Subjected to Torture and Other Cruel, Inhuman or Degrading Treatment or Punishment has been abbreviated to the UN Declaration against Torture. The European Convention for the Protection of Human Rights and Fundamental Freedoms has been abbreviated to the European Convention on Human Rights.

INTRODUCTION

LONDON, Friday, 16 October 1998, British police arrest Augusto Pinochet, former military ruler of Chile. The news of Augusto Pinochet's detention in the United Kingdom (UK) was celebrated around the world. Why? Because for millions of people the former Chilean ruler's name was a byword for torture, killings and political repression. Although Augusto Pinochet was eventually allowed to return to Chile on health grounds in March 2000, his arrest transformed the human rights landscape. It affirmed that even those who had governed their countries with absolute power were no longer immune from prosecution.

For more than 25 years following the violent coup that brought Augusto Pinochet to power, Chilean human rights activists continued their courageous struggle to see the torturers brought to account. For Veronica de Negri, the long journey in pursuit of justice took her to the public gallery of the House of Lords in London in 1999 to witness the proceedings against Augusto Pinochet.

Veronica de Negri was tortured by the Chilean secret service in 1975. A former Communist Party activist, she was beaten and raped at a naval base near Valparaiso and a concentration camp in the capital Santiago. "The abuse was physical and mental... They did unspeakable things with rats, as well as little things, like denying me tampons. I find the details painful to recall." In 1977 Veronica fled the country.

Nine years later, in July 1986, her son Rodrigo became another victim of the Chilean security forces. Torture under Augusto Pinochet had moved beyond the interrogation chamber into the streets. "I was tortured for months and survived. Rodrigo was tortured for 10 minutes and he died."

Rodrigo Rojas de Negri and his friend Carmen Quintana were walking down a street in a poor suburb of Santiago when they were rounded up by a Chilean army patrol. The soldiers dragged them into a side street and started beating them, breaking their bones. According to Carmen, who survived the attack, some 30 men were involved. In front of eyewitnesses, the soldiers doused Carmen and

Women demonstrate in Dhaka, Bangladesh, demanding an end to "torture, cruelty and repression" against women, August 1997.

Rodrigo in kerosene and set them alight. The soldiers then wrapped their charred bodies in blankets and dumped them in a ditch. By the time Veronica was able to see Rodrigo in hospital he was just hours from death; the only way she could communicate with him was by rubbing the soles of his feet.

What was the response of the authorities? When 6,000 people attended Rodrigo's funeral in Santiago, riot police fired water cannon at the mourners. Augusto Pinochet himself went on national television to deny any army involvement in the burnings, despite all the evidence to the contrary. Eventually, and under pressure, he appointed a special judge to investigate; the judge absolved the army patrol of blame. Only the leader of the patrol has ever been prosecuted — for "negligence".

Efforts to hold Augusto Pinochet accountable for the many crimes of torture committed by his regime continue. The challenge to his impunity comes after 25 years in which much has been achieved in the struggle against torture. A global human rights movement has emerged, and, largely thanks to its efforts, numerous new international standards have been adopted prohibiting torture and setting out governments' obligations to prevent it. An impressive array of international human rights mechanisms has been put in place to press states to live up to their commitments.

Despite these advances, torturers continue to inflict physical agony and mental anguish on countless victims — and to get away with it. While the torturers evade accountability, the wounds of their victims cannot heal and society is poisoned from within.

This report launches a new Amnesty International (AI) campaign against torture. It examines the reasons why torture persists. It explores avenues for achieving the goal of eradicating torture and other cruel, inhuman or degrading treatment or punishment (ill-treatment). In preparing this report, AI conducted a survey of its research files on 195 countries and territories. The survey covered the period from the beginning of 1997 to mid-2000. Information on torture is usually concealed, and reports are often hard to document, so the figures presented in this report almost certainly underestimate the extent of torture.

The statistics are shocking. There were reports of torture or ill-treatment by state officials in more than 150 countries. In more

TAKE A STEP TO STAMP OUT TORTURE

A Togolese woman fleeing torture in her country waits for news of her asylum application in a US county jail, December 1998. Many of the world's 15 million refugees are torture victims.

than 70, they were widespread or persistent. In more than 80 countries, people reportedly died as a result. The evidence strongly suggests that most of the victims were people suspected or convicted of criminal offences. Most of the torturers were police officers.

In the light of this grim evidence, the urgency of the task ahead is undeniable. Every human being has the right to live free from the threat of torture. States must move beyond paper pledges to implement international human rights law and deliver the protection it promises. Governments must be held to account. Those in authority must be forced to honour their commitments.

The law is unequivocal – torture is absolutely prohibited in all circumstances. However, the very people charged with implementing the law frequently flout it. Some governments use torture as part of their strategy for holding on to power. Many more pay lip service to human rights, but their rhetoric conceals a profound lack of political will to hold torturers to account. Around the world, the people who inflict torture commit their crimes with impunity. More than any other single factor, impunity sends the message that torture – although illegal – will be tolerated.

The world has changed immeasurably since AI first began denouncing torture at the height of the Cold War in the 1960s. The challenges and opportunities facing the fight against torture have also evolved. It is clear that torture is not confined to military dictatorships or authoritarian regimes; torture is inflicted in democratic states too. It is also clear that the victims of torture are criminal suspects as well as political prisoners, the disadvantaged as well as the dissident, people targeted because of their identity as well as their beliefs. They are women as well as men, children as well as adults.

As a result of the work of women's movements around the world over the past four decades, there is now greater awareness of the abuse women experience in everyday life, such as rape and domestic violence. This has given increased impetus to the demand that governments fulfil their responsibilities to prevent and punish torture whether inflicted by state officials or by private individuals.

Technological developments have influenced both the means of inflicting torture and the possibilities for combating it. Electro-shock devices have been developed to restrain, control or punish. At the same time communications technology means that anti-torture campaigners can organize in new ways. Today it is harder for torturers to hide; new international activist networks and coalitions can pursue them wherever they go.

Cases of torture can become headline news the world over within hours. Millions of people have been exposed to the reality of torture through the media. For the witnesses to the pain and suffering of fellow human beings, this knowledge brings responsibility. A responsibility to do everything possible — as individuals, professionals or members of our communities — to bring the eradication of torture one step closer.

> "Methods of torture include: stretching the body on a ladder; suspension from the wrists; electric shocks; pulling out the finger nails; dripping acid on the feet; the insertion of a broken bottle into the anus; prolonged flogging... We have, or have seen those who have, all experienced such blind methods of torture. Bodies of some took years to recover from the effects of torture, but the bodies of others have permanent disabilities."
> **Letter smuggled out of a Syrian prison in January 2000**

An Indian police officer wielding a lathi (long wooden stick) approaches a child searching for food at Chowpatti Beach, Bombay.

In the last few years, ground-breaking measures have been taken to ensure that alleged torturers who evade justice in their own country can be held to account internationally. Significant steps have been taken towards establishing the International Criminal Court to try cases of torture and other international crimes against humanity. The arrests of Hissein Habré, former ruler of Chad, in Senegal to face charges of human rights abuses including torture, and of Augusto Pinochet in the UK, illustrate a greater willingness by courts to bring torturers to justice wherever they may be, although both cases also show the ability of political officials to impede the course of justice.

For all that the world around us has changed, the persistence of torture at this moment in history calls into question the very notion of human progress. It is an indictment of the collective failure of governments to honour the pledge they made more than 50 years ago in the Universal Declaration of Human Rights — "No one shall be subjected to torture or to cruel, inhuman or degrading treatment or punishment."[1]

This report does not attempt only to describe the problem of torture today. It also sets out a strategy for eradicating it.

AI's new campaign — **Take a step to stamp out torture** — seeks to galvanize people around the world in a collective effort to eradicate torture. The campaign builds on AI's experience over four decades of researching and working against torture. AI, with its million-plus members, aims to collaborate with human rights organizations, trade unions, community organizations and concerned individuals in order to strengthen the global anti-torture network.

The campaign's strategy is to achieve progress in three major areas — preventing torture, confronting discrimination and overcoming impunity.

There is no shortage of information on how to prevent torture. Procedures, laws and international conventions have been elaborated which governments can use to reduce the likelihood of torture. AI's 12-Point Program for the Prevention of Torture by Agents of the State (see Appendix 1) brings together the most important measures for preventing torture in custody. In this campaign AI aims to challenge political leaders around the world to declare their opposition to torture and to implement these measures. AI sections, groups and members around the world will intensify their work to raise awareness of torture and how to stop it. National strategies to combat torture are being developed and implemented by AI and partner organizations in more than 20 countries. The insights gained and the links forged during the campaign will, it is hoped, serve the fight against torture for years to come.

This campaign seeks to highlight the links between discrimination and torture, and calls on governments to take action to combat discrimination. Torture involves dehumanizing the victim and this dehumanization is made easier if the victims come from a disadvantaged social, political or ethnic group. AI activists around the world will focus on confronting violence against women that constitutes torture, lobbying for action against torture at the UN World Conference on Racism in 2001, working to end the torture of children, and campaigning against the torture of lesbian, gay, bisexual and transgendered people.

Impunity is one of the main factors which allow torture to continue. Impunity undermines the systems built up over the years to protect against torture. When society's defences are down, any opportunistic pretext — such as the need to combat "terrorism", the fight against crime, or hostility to groups such as asylum-seekers — may be used as a licence to torture. If torturers

An orphan on Peace Street in the Chechen capital, Grozny, 1996. In modern conflicts, terrorizing civilian populations has become a common means of waging war. This almost invariably involves torture.

are not brought to justice, it encourages others to believe that torture can be committed with impunity. It also prevents victims and their families from establishing the truth and denies them justice. AI sections will campaign in their countries to ensure that national legislation provides for torturers to be brought to justice, either by prosecution or extradition to stand trial in another country. The campaign also seeks to strengthen international mechanisms to ensure that those responsible for torture are brought to justice.

We have waited too long for governments to honour their commitment to end torture. The campaign against torture has to be led by ordinary people. It is time for human rights activists and their supporters to join forces to step up the fight against torture and hold governments accountable. The prevalence of torture can seem daunting, but a campaign founded on unity in action has the potential to empower and motivate. Torturers thrive on the indifference of the general public. Our task must be to turn indifference into outrage and outrage into action.

1: TORTURE TODAY

"I must confess... I do not have the words or expressions to convey to you precisely the horrors that I lived through...

"I was taken, blindfolded, to the entrance to my cell where the "Panther"[2] was waiting for me... He took off the blindfold and started beating me... I was stripped naked and taken into a small room, about three metres square; more than 30 people were crowded into the room. This was where I learned what human beings can do to one another...

- imagine for a moment a hot iron being put on my stomach
- imagine the kind of scissors used by hairdressers... used to tear the skin from my back, right to the shoulder blade, as if my skin were a piece of fabric
- imagine the kind of pincers used by car mechanics or scrap merchants – the "Panther" used them to pull out my finger nails as my fellow inmates looked on helplessly
- imagine being forced to drink other people's urine, a Kalashnikov held to my throat...
- imagine... a small table knife with a serrated blade which they use to pierce my tongue. You can still see the scar...

"One fine day a man arrives... and says 'You're Adrien Wayi aren't you?... tonight at 2 o'clock in the morning you're going on a journey, without a passport. You'll be killed in the Makala camp and then thrown into the river like the others... Understand?'

"I understood that a man is frightened when he hopes he will be saved. I had lost all hope of living and was no longer afraid of dying. The only thing I regretted was that I would not have a grave where my children could remember me..."

Kenyan police assaulting a protester in Nairobi, July 1997. Several peaceful pro-democracy rallies were violently disrupted during the run-up to elections in 1997 by police using batons, tear gas and water cannon.

Journalist Adrien Wayi was held for 12 days in October 1997 in the Bacongo area of Brazzaville by one of the warring militias in the Republic of the Congo. He was arrested because of his links with one of the militia leaders. The scars on his back, his tongue and his wrists are still visible. But not all his scars are physical; he continues to suffer memory loss, difficulties with his hearing and vision and severe headaches. He has difficulty sleeping, not only because of the nightmares, but also because his injuries mean it is still too painful for him to lie on his back.

Adrien Wayi's experiences show how torturers continue to devise countless different ways of inflicting pain. They use violence and terror to extract information or coerce a confession; to break down an individual physically and mentally; to terrorize particular groups or whole communities; to punish or humiliate individuals.

The effects of torture reverberate far beyond the suffering of the individual victims. The consequences on the immediate family, on the community and on society as a whole are both profound and long-lived. For the survivors the worst consequences are often psychological. Many are haunted by deep feelings of guilt and shame: guilt that they have survived while others have not, shame that information they gave under torture may have harmed friends. Others faced with an "impossible choice" – reveal the names of comrades or watch a loved one being tortured – continue to feel responsible for the

Methods of torture

Beating is by far the most common method of torture and ill-treatment used by state officials today. Reports of beating have been received from more than 150 countries – virtually all the countries from which torture and ill-treatment have been reported since 1997. Common methods of torture and ill-treatment reported since 1997 include electric shocks (more than 40 countries), rape and sexual abuse in custody (more than 50 countries), suspension of the body (more than 40 countries), beating on the soles of the feet (more than 30 countries), suffocation (more than 30 countries), mock execution or threat of death (more than 50 countries) and prolonged solitary confinement (more than 50 countries). Other methods included submersion in water, stubbing out of cigarettes on the body, being tied to the back of a car and dragged behind it, sleep deprivation and sensory deprivation.

TAKE A STEP TO STAMP OUT TORTURE

A Congolese militiaman undergoing ritual humiliation while in training for the new national army. In many countries military recruits, in particular those in the lower ranks, are vulnerable to brutal treatment and are often subjected to routine abuse, both physical and mental.

outcome long after the physical scars left by the torturer have healed.

Language can disguise the horror of torture and render the most horrific acts unremarkable. Beatings are the most widespread form of torture or ill-treatment. The word may sound fairly banal: the reality is not. People are beaten with fists, sticks, gun-butts, makeshift whips, iron pipes, baseball bats, electric flex… the list goes on. The victims suffer bruises, internal bleeding, broken bones, lost teeth, ruptured organs. Some die.

Other forms of torture may leave fewer marks on the body — near suffocation, being kept with a hood over the head, mock execution, sleep deprivation and exposure to extremes of heat or cold — but can be just as destructive of the human body and personality as electric shocks or battering. Prolonged standing, for example, eventually causes swelling of the legs, circulation problems, hallucinations and kidney failure. Some innocent-sounding "instruments of restraint" can, if used for long periods, cause blood clots, permanent disability, even death.

AI's first campaigns against torture were fuelled by the outrage of people around the world at the treatment meted out to prisoners of conscience — the "forgotten victims" languishing in jail. Not only were these people being incarcerated for what they believed; they were being tortured and ill-treated in order to force them to abandon their views and to deter them from their struggle. Torture continues to be used as an instrument of political repression. In many parts of the world, those who challenge the prevailing order, whether non-violently or by taking up arms, are still likely targets of torture and ill-treatment.

However, AI's global survey into patterns of torture today strongly suggests that the most common victims of torture and ill-treatment are convicted criminals and criminal suspects. The torture of these people has not so far sparked a great deal of popular mobilization to oppose it. There are a number of reasons for this. The prevalence of torture against criminal suspects may be under-reported, as the victims generally have less access to complaint mechanisms. Beatings of criminal suspects may be so routine that they are not recognized as torture, even by the victims themselves. In some countries, long-standing torture of common criminals has only attracted attention once levels of more overt political repression have waned. The perpetrators, and indeed the public, may see violence against criminal suspects as "criminals getting what they deserve". Such violence is sometimes advocated by those who wish to see tougher action against rising crime. In the absence of proper training and investigative resources, police may resort to torture or ill-treatment as "short-cut methods" to extract confessions and gain convictions. Criminal suspects will almost invariably be from the poorest or most marginalized sectors of society. Discrimination against such groups often contributes to the lack of action against their torture or ill-treatment. In many countries, beatings and other physical and psychological abuse are standard practice for arrested criminal suspects or marginalized individuals who come into contact with the law. In some cases, the purpose is to extract information, or to

Footage, captured by a hidden camera, showing a criminal suspect being handcuffed to the window bar of a Shanghai police station, China, April 1998.

obtain a "confession", true or false. In others, punishment and humiliation appear to be the primary aim.

Torture is often committed by police officers, soldiers, intelligence officers, prison guards or other agents of the state. But not always. Torture can also be inflicted by members of armed political groups or, in some circumstances, by private individuals.

Torture cannot be defined by a list of prohibited practices. It is equally impossible to draw a clear dividing line between "torture" and other "cruel, inhuman or degrading treatment or punishment". Whether an act of ill-treatment constitutes torture depends on a number of factors including the nature and severity of the abuse. Both torture and ill-treatment are prohibited by international law, but the international legal mechanisms for dealing with torture are stronger.

Torture has been defined in a number of international treaties. The definitions vary, reflecting the different contexts in which they were drafted, and the purposes of the treaties in which they appear.

UN Convention against Torture

Article 1: "For the purposes of this Convention, the term "torture" means any act by which severe pain or suffering, whether physical or mental, is intentionally inflicted on a person for such purposes as obtaining from him or a third person information or a confession, punishing him for an act he or a third person has committed or is suspected of having committed, or intimidating or coercing him or a third person, or for any reason based on discrimination of any kind, when such pain or suffering is inflicted by or at the instigation of or with the consent or acquiescence of a public official or other person acting in an official capacity. It does not include pain or suffering arising only from, inherent in or incidental to lawful sanctions."

The UN Convention against Torture, adopted in 1984, is one of the least ratified major human rights treaties. Only 119 states had ratified the Convention by mid-2000 (see Appendix 3). Only 41 states had made declarations under Article 22 of the Convention so as to allow individuals in their countries to raise complaints of torture with the Committee against Torture established under the Convention. Only 44 had made declarations under Article 21 allowing for inter-state complaints. Seven states had made reservations exempting them from the procedure for a confidential inquiry into allegations of systematic torture as set out in Article 20. Many states had made other reservations.

Egypt

> "I said that I would write and sign anything they wanted me to... I signed those papers... Then they took me outside the building and let me go."
>
> Amal Farouq Mohammad al-Maas

Amal Farouq Mohammad al-Maas was interrogated and tortured by officers of the State Security Investigations Department (SSI) for the first time in Cairo on 26 April 1993. The officers reportedly made her undress, tied her hands and feet and suspended her from a bar, beat her repeatedly with a rubber hose and a stick, blindfolded her, and threatened to rape her. At times she could hear her husband, Ahmad Mohammad Ahmad al-Sayyid, who had been arrested earlier that day, screaming in another room.

After roughly 24 hours of interrogation Amal Farouq Mohammad al-Maas signed a statement saying that SSI officers had found weapons and explosives at the couple's home; she was released immediately. The statement was reportedly used by a military court, during a trial held in May 1993, to convict her husband and sentence him to 25 years' imprisonment.

After her release, Amal Farouq Mohammad al-Maas filed a complaint with the Director of the Prosecution Office in al-Doqqi district, Cairo, about her torture at the SSI branch in Gaber bin Hayyan Street. She was interviewed at length on 4 May 1993 and a forensic medical report, issued on 8 May 1993, concluded that her injuries were consistent with her allegations of torture.

In September 1993 the Director of the Prosecution Office in al-Doqqi summoned two SSI officers, identified by Amal Farouq Mohammad al-Maas as her torturers, to come to the Prosecution Office for investigation. They failed to present themselves and ignored 56 subsequent summonses. In January 1996, one officer responded to the summons, but denied the allegations. Later that month, the SSI denied that anyone named Amal Farouq Mohammad al-Maas had been held at the SSI branch in Gaber bin Hayyan Street between 26 and 28 April 1993.

In July 1996 SSI officers rearrested Amal Farouq Mohammad al-Maas and took her to an SSI branch in al-Marsa district to try to coerce her into withdrawing her complaint. They reportedly slashed her arms, back and legs with a sharp knife, blindfolded her, suspended her from the ceiling by one arm for two hours, and gave her electric shocks. After 10 days of torture, the SSI officers dumped her, unconscious, in the street. Amal Farouq Mohammad al-Maas' attempts to file subsequent complaints have been unsuccessful.

In October 1999 Amal Farouq Mohammad al-Maas was contacted by a television company to arrange an interview about her treatment in detention. The night before the interview was due to take place, SSI officers telephoned her to ask why she wanted to give the interview. They came to her house early the next morning, "bugged" the rooms with surveillance equipment and threatened her with arrest. When the television company arrived Amal Farouq Mohammad al-Maas was unable to continue with the interview.

Amal Farouq Mohammad al-Maas' experience was not an isolated one. In May 1999 the UN Committee against Torture expressed its concern about the "treatment of female detainees, by both the police and the State Security Intelligence, which sometimes involves sexual abuse or threats in order to obtain information relating to husbands or other family members".

Register to take action against torture at www.stoptorture.org

AMAL FAROUQ MOHAMMAD AL-MAAS

The UN Convention against Torture definition of torture refers to an "act by which severe pain or suffering, whether physical or mental, is intentionally inflicted on a person", for a purpose such as obtaining information or a confession, punishment, intimidation or coercion, "or for any reason based on discrimination of any kind". The Convention is concerned with torture by government agents or people acting with official sanction.

The Inter-American Convention to Prevent and Punish Torture defines torture more broadly than the UN Convention. It includes as torture "the use of methods upon a person intended to obliterate the personality of the victim or to diminish his physical or mental capacities, even if they do not cause physical pain or mental anguish".

Human rights treaties define torture in broad terms. The task of interpreting the definitions in practice — and ensuring that they are applied consistently — falls to various inter-governmental bodies which monitor states' compliance with the relevant international treaties. These monitoring bodies, as well as national courts, continually make decisions which refine and develop the interpretation of what constitutes torture — international human rights treaties are "living instruments", evolving and developing over time.

Because AI works primarily to combat human rights abuses by states and armed opposition groups, this report focuses on such situations. The terms "torture" and "ill-treatment" are therefore used here to refer to acts involving the infliction of pain or suffering by state agents, or similar acts by private individuals for which the state bears responsibility through consent, acquiescence or inaction. Torture and ill-treatment also refers to similar acts inflicted by members of armed political groups.

The understanding of what constitutes torture is not fixed for all time. The enduring image of torture in the popular imagination is that of the political prisoner in the interrogation chamber. But torture and ill-treatment are inflicted on a much broader range of people than is generally realized. Torture is committed not just in the police station or prison cell. Not just in the army barracks or in the rebel encampment. Torture is committed in all these places, but also in juvenile detention centres, refugee camps, on the streets and in people's homes. Strategies for eradicating torture have to reflect this developing understanding of the variety of contexts in which torture is inflicted.

Torture at the hands of the police

"They beat him every night, especially on the soles of his feet. His right leg was completely raw, it was infected, his foot swelled up. On 24 January, at about six in the evening, some of the prisoners asked the guards to take him out of the cell so that he wouldn't infect the others. A policeman replied: 'In any case, we're going to kill you all'. Bessy was dying, he stank. At half past seven he stopped moving and a quarter of an hour later he still hadn't moved."
A detainee describes the death of a Nigerian called Bessy, one of six detainees who died in a police cell in Equatorial Guinea in early 1998.

Torture or ill-treatment by police officers has been reported in more than 140 countries since 1997. Police officers are responsible for upholding the law and protecting the rights of all members of society. However, police officers are by far the most common state agents of torture. Many of the victims come into contact with the law because they are suspected of committing a crime, others are members of groups targeted by prejudiced police forces. Often those most at risk of police abuse are members of racial or ethnic minorities. In most countries the number of prosecutions for police brutality represents only a tiny fraction of the number of complaints made; convictions are rarer still.

In China, home to a fifth of humanity, torture and ill-treatment of detainees and prisoners is commonplace. Victims have included many people who became involved in disputes with officials by questioning their authority or by attempting to uphold their own rights. Torture as part of blackmail and extortion by corrupt police officers is frequently reported. Migrant workers, particularly young women far from the protection of family and community, are frequent victims. Torture during interrogation is perpetrated against all types of detainees. Reports of torture increase during periodic "strike

Indonesian police attack a student demonstrator in Jakarta in June 2000. Despite some progress towards reform in Indonesia, torture and ill-treatment of both political and criminal suspects continue to be widespread.

hard" campaigns against specific crimes, when police are clearly given the green light to use "every means" to achieve "quick results". Torture and ill-treatment are also a component part of some high-profile political campaigns such as the crack-down on the banned *Falun Gong* spiritual movement. The authorities have completely failed to investigate and prosecute alleged torture in such cases.

Many people die in custody each year in China as a result of torture. For example, between September 1999 and June 2000 at least 13 *Falun Gong* practitioners died in police custody, some reportedly as a result of torture. Zhao Jinhua, a farmer from Zhaojia village, Shandong province, was seized by Zhangxing town police on 27 September 1999 while she was working in the fields. She died in a police station in Zhangxing town on 7 October 1999. In police custody she was reportedly beaten with clubs and electro-shock batons when she refused to renounce the *Falun Gong*. An autopsy found that death had been caused by beatings with blunt instruments, but her body was cremated immediately afterwards. The authorities subsequently claimed she had died of heart failure.

Often the primary aim of police brutality is to extract a confession or to punish an individual. Twelve-year-old Halil

Ibrahim Okkalı ended up in intensive care after being interrogated in Çinarli Police Station in Izmir, Turkey, in November 1995. He was suspected of a theft. Halil Ibrahim Okkalı reported that he was questioned by two policemen who took him to the toilet where they beat him with a truncheon and kicked him after he fell on the floor. The torture allegations were pursued through the courts, but the police commissioner convicted of torturing Halil Ibrahim Okkalı was promoted to chief commissioner during the course of the trial. He was sentenced, together with another officer, to a fine and suspension from duty for two months in October 1996. The Appeal Court overturned the verdict and, after a retrial, the officers were each given a 10-month prison sentence in February 1998, confirmed by the Appeal Court in March 1999. These sentences were suspended. Meanwhile, Halil Ibrahim Okkalı still suffers from the effects of the torture inflicted on him.

Reliance on information obtained under torture as a routine method of criminal investigation is more prevalent in countries where police are not given adequate training or resources, or where police are encouraged to use "strong methods" against suspected criminals in response to high levels of crime.

Difficulties in implementing crucial reforms to the criminal justice system in South Africa have meant that members of the security forces continue to resort to methods of criminal investigation associated with the *apartheid* era, despite the prohibition of torture in the Constitution. Current high levels of violent crime in the country have encouraged public support for harsh measures against suspected or convicted criminals. For example, Military Police officers assaulted Zweli Kenneth Ndlozi in his home in Soweto in front of eyewitnesses in September 1998. They accused him of involvement in the theft of firearms, searched the house for weapons, then took him away. Two days later, his family were informed by police that he had been found dead in a cell at Germiston police station, hanging by a nylon cord around his neck. An independent post-mortem examination found serious injuries unrelated to his apparent death by hanging, notably lesions consistent with cigarette burns as well as evidence of a severe blow to the head. More than 200 deaths in police custody were reported in 1998, some allegedly as a result of torture or ill-treatment.

La Paz, Bolivia, 1998. Security forces in full riot gear confront striking teachers and other public sector workers. At least 10 people were killed and dozens more injured when the police and army opened fire on strikers demonstrating in La Paz and El Chapare in April 1998. Children and teachers were among the victims.

Not all police torture and ill-treatment are committed in the course of criminal investigations; they can occur when police use excessive force in the name of maintaining public order. In Zambia, in August 1997, street vendors protested after their stalls were burned down by unknown arsonists in the makeshift "Soweto Market" in downtown Lusaka. Hundreds of heavily armed paramilitary police officers began to beat both protesters and uninvolved passers-by with batons and fired tear gas canisters at groups of people found in the downtown area. Jane Mwamba, a vendor who was caught up in the police assault with her baby, told a local newspaper that she was watching the damage caused by the fire with several other women when the police fired tear gas canisters at them. "While trying to run, I fell down and a policeman came and kicked me repeatedly to an extent where I could not walk." There were allegations by some witnesses that police were so brutal that two protesters were beaten to death.

Although the police are authorized to use force in carrying out their duties, international standards place strict limits on the extent to which force may be used. According to the UN Code of Conduct for Law Enforcement Officials and the UN Basic Principles on the Use of Force and Firearms by Law Enforcement Officials, police officers may use force only when strictly necessary, and to the

Brazil

Fifteen-year-old José (not his real name) was arrested in June 1999 and held for two days. During that time he was beaten so severely by civil police officers that he has needed psychiatric treatment ever since. Latest reports indicate that José is also still receiving treatment for damage to his testicles as a result of the beatings.

José left his home in Xinguara, Pará state, on the afternoon of 7 June to go to a bingo hall with friends. His mother, Iraci Oliveira dos Santos, became concerned when he did not return that night and searched for him in local hospitals before going to the police station where she was told he had been detained.

After waiting for several hours, she was eventually allowed to see José on the evening of 8 June. She says she found him in great pain and covered in bruises. One of the other boys being held told her that José had been badly treated both inside and outside the police station and that she should take her son away as soon as possible.

José told his mother that he had been followed by the police when he left home, and had become scared and fallen off his motorbike. The police stopped, aimed their guns at him, kicked him and threatened to kill him. They drove him to an unknown location where they beat and threatened him again. Finally he was taken to the police station, accused of possessing a small amount of cannabis and a small handgun. In the evening, the police took José into the corridor of the police station and beat him once again. Other boys held in the police station said that the beating was so severe they thought he would be killed. José was forced to confess to previous arrests which had not taken place.

On 9 June Iraci Oliveira dos Santos tried to speak to the Police Chief about her son's detention, but he refused to see her, saying that she had been impolite to his officers. The police let her know through a friend that she could take her son home if she agreed not to make a complaint about his treatment. Anxious to get medical treatment for her son, she agreed.

IRACI OLIVEIRA DOS SANTOS WAS BRAVE ENOUGH TO BRING THE TORTURE OF HER SON TO PUBLIC ATTENTION.

Since his release José has suffered from psychological problems and has been admitted to a psychiatric institution on several occasions for periods of one or two months. After the new year holiday, which he spent with his family, his mental condition worsened dramatically. He was readmitted to the psychiatric hospital on 16 February 2000 and remains a patient there.

Although José was released from police custody on condition that Iraci Oliveira dos Santos did not complain about her son's treatment, she has since made a formal complaint to the Public Prosecutor. The Public Prosecutor has referred the case for investigation to the same Police Chief in charge of the police station where José was tortured. Iraci Oliveira dos Santos is so appalled at the treatment received by her son that she has taken the rare – and brave – step of publicizing the case in Brazil and appearing on television. There have been widespread reports of police brutality in Xinguara, of which very few have been investigated, often because survivors and witnesses have been too frightened to come forward.

Register to take action against torture at www.stoptorture.org

minimum extent required in the circumstances. As far as possible they should employ non-violent means before resorting to the use of force. Officers are required to exercise restraint and act in proportion to the seriousness of the offence and the legitimate objective to be achieved.

Cruel, inhuman or degrading conditions of detention

"This place is worse than a pigsty. The water tanks are in such bad condition that disease spreads at an alarming rate, even affecting the local community who live near the prison. Solitary confinement is used indiscriminately. You'd be lucky to get out alive: conditions here pose serious risks to the mental and physical health of the prisoners, quite apart from the torture inflicted by completely untrained prison officers."

This extract is taken from a letter passed to AI from prisoners in the Roger prison in João Pessoa, Paraíba, Brazil, in April 1998, after AI delegates were prevented from entering and speaking to prisoners. It describes conditions and treatment typical of the situations taken up by AI – an unhealthy living environment, lack of medical care and arbitrary application of punishment. Life in such prisons is unhealthy, degrading and dangerous. Protests, jail breaks and violent confrontations are often the result.

Torture, ill-treatment and deliberate neglect are rife behind the prison walls of many countries. For some prisoners, they combine to turn a prison sentence into a death sentence.

When asked what are their most acute problems, prisoners generally cite overcrowding, lack of food and medical care, inadequate sanitation, violence, arbitrary punishment and denial of contact with family. In those cases where conditions are so bad as to amount to cruel, inhuman or degrading treatment, there is almost always a combination of these elements at work.

Some governments cite lack of resources as the reason why they cannot improve conditions in prisons and other places of detention. However, if the political will is there, any government can improve conditions in key areas. Some improvements, such as allowing family visits, access to reading materials or longer periods

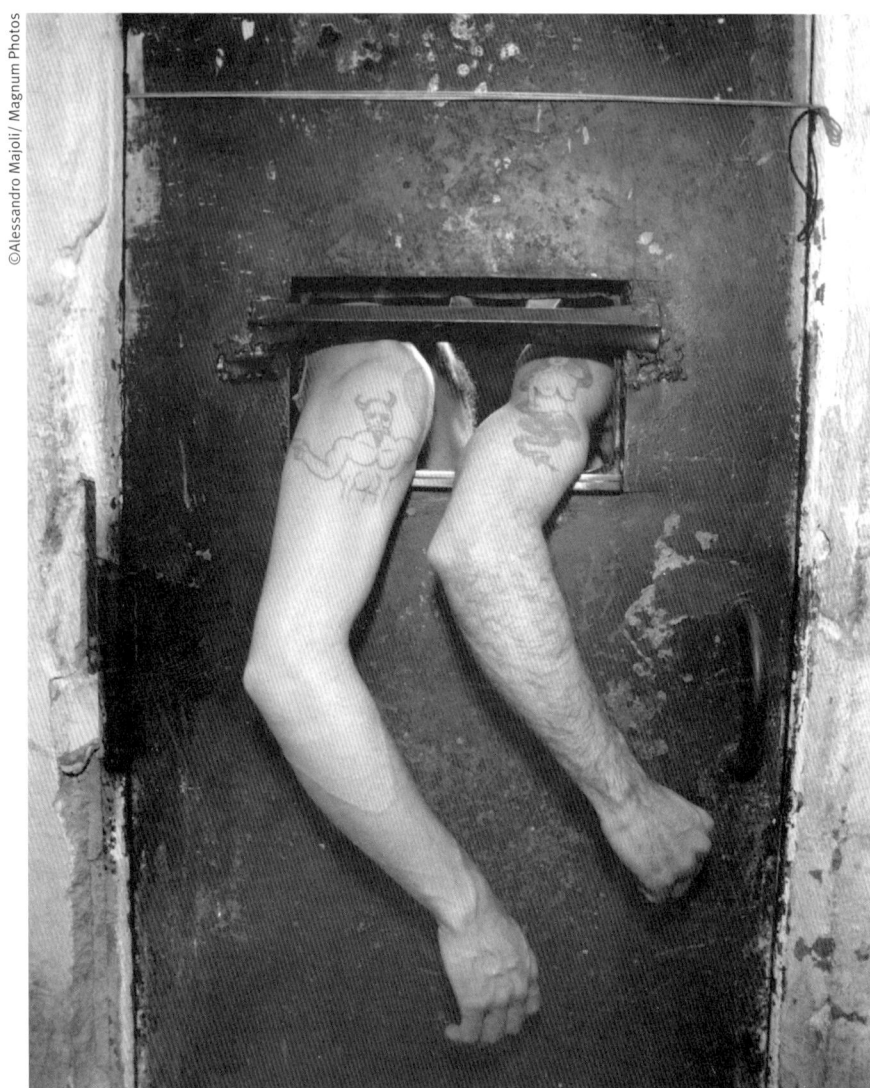

©Alessandro Majoli/ Magnum Photos

outside cells, are virtually cost free. Others, such as reforms to the criminal justice system, are part of good governance, as well as a way to address chronic overcrowding.

In the USA, the most powerful economy in the world, some facilities have been starved of funds and are overcrowded and understaffed, creating dangerous and inhuman conditions. In many, violence is endemic. In some cases guards fail to stop inmates assaulting each other. In others the guards

Carandiru Prison, São Paulo, Brazil, is one of the world's largest prisons. It holds approximately 7,000 prisoners but there are only 100 guards.

> According to AI's survey, conditions of detention amounting to cruel, inhuman or degrading treatment were reported in 90 countries and were widespread in more than 50 countries.

themselves are the abusers, subjecting their victims to beatings and sexual abuse. In recent years a new type of prison, built at great expense, has created a different set of concerns. In so-called "supermaximum security" (or "supermax") facilities, prisoners are subjected to extreme isolation and sensory deprivation. They typically spend between 22 and 24 hours a day confined to small, solitary cells in which they eat, sleep and defecate. The Human Rights Committee, the expert body which monitors the implementation of the International Covenant on Civil and Political Rights, stated in 1995 that conditions in certain US maximum security prisons were "incompatible" with the requirement in Article 10 of the Covenant. This provides that anyone deprived of their liberty "shall be treated with humanity and respect for the inherent dignity of the human person".

The effects of long-term isolation can be highly destructive. A former prisoner held in prolonged solitary confinement in South Korea (Republic of Korea) told AI after her release in 1997: "In my third year of imprisonment I could not remember the names of close friends and family and easy everyday conversational vocabulary. I had difficulty speaking during visiting hours. I tried to read aloud and sing for at least an hour every day, but I would soon lose my voice..."

A prisoner in leg chains being forced to cut stones for road building near Toungoo, Myanmar, where forced labour is common, January 2000.

The UN Standard Minimum Rules for the Treatment of Prisoners set out detailed rules for the treatment of prisoners and detainees. There are also international standards

140 prisoners in a cell designed for 35 at a pre-trial detention centre near Moscow in August 1995. More than a million people are being held in grossly overcrowded, pest-ridden and badly ventilated Russian prisons where food and medical treatment is often inadequate.

governing the treatment of particular groups such as children. Not every breach of these rules would necessarily amount to cruel, inhuman or degrading treatment. In the situations which AI takes up, where the state has failed in its responsibility to ensure freedom from torture and ill-treatment, the breaches of these rules are either multiple or particularly severe.

Any criminal justice system is vulnerable to the pressures of politics, economics or prejudice. Blaming criminal suspects and convicted prisoners for society's ills can feed public indifference to their plight in prison. But the right not to be tortured or ill-treated does not end at the prison gates. Any erosion of fundamental human rights for some undermines the rights of all.

"Lawful torture": judicial corporal punishment

When governments are accused of committing torture or ill-treatment, the most usual response is denial. Denial that the event took place; denial that they knew; or denial that they were responsible. Corporal punishment of prisoners is one of the few exceptions. These punishments are imposed by courts as a penal sanction or by administrative order as a disciplinary measure. They are carried out by state officials, sometimes in public, and

Judicial corporal punishments

Since 1997 AI has documented cases of judicial floggings in 14 countries and amputations in seven. Judicial corporal punishments are currently on the statute books of at least 31 countries. Judicial corporal punishments have been abolished or declared unconstitutional in four countries since 1997 (Jamaica, St. Vincent and the Grenadines, South Africa and Zambia) and introduced in one country (Nigeria).

Country	Amputations inflicted 1997 to 2000	Floggings inflicted 1997 to 2000	Judicial corporal punishment provided in law as at June 2000
Afghanistan	●		●
Antigua and Barbuda			●
Bahamas			●
Barbados			●
Bermuda			●
Botswana			●
Brunei Darussalam			●
Fiji			●
Grenada			●
Guyana			●
Iran	●		●
Iraq	●		●
Kenya		●	●
Libya			●
Malaysia		●	●
Nigeria	●	●	●
Pakistan		●	●
Russian Federation (Chechen Republic)	●		●
Saint Kitts & Nevis			●
Saint Lucia			●
Saudi Arabia	●	●	●
Singapore		●	●
Somalia	●	●	●
Sri Lanka		●	●
Sudan	●	●	●
Tanzania		●	●
Trinidad and Tobago		●	●
Uganda		●	●
United Arab Emirates			●
Yemen		●	●
Zimbabwe		●	●

Laos

> "I am seriously ill... I can't eat anything. I can't sleep. I am groaning with pain all the time."
>
> **Feng Sakchittaphong**

LATSAMI KHAMPHOUI

Feng Sakchittaphong and Latsami Khamphoui are both suffering from angina and kidney problems, but they have no hope of receiving the medical attention they desperately need. Government officials and police officers have even confiscated medication which was sent to them by relatives. The two 60-year-old men have spent more than seven years at Prison Camp 7 in Houa Phanh, a remote province in the northeast of the country, where conditions are extremely harsh. Contact with family members is tightly restricted and intervals between permitted visits have lasted for up to two years.

In March 1998 a letter from one of the prisoners reached Amnesty International. It was dated January 1998 and it stated: "...the dictatorial authorities are using schemes of incommunicado detention, including prohibitions on family visits and the total denial of all medical care... This overall situation is the reason why we have now fallen into double ill health and deterioration... On 11 January 1998 the Head of the Prison 7 came personally to inspect the poor state of our health. He thus knew the facts of how truly poorly we were... We then asked about our food ration, because for the past three or four months we had only low quality rice, and none of us would be able to withstand this any longer, this endless deprivation..."

Less than one month later, Thongsouk Saysangkhi, a friend and fellow prison inmate of Feng Sakchittaphong and

FENG SAKCHITTAPHONG

Latsami Khamphoui, died. He too had suffered from angina and kidney problems.

Amnesty International had consistently warned the Lao authorities that the three men required urgent medical treatment. These warnings were ignored and Thongsouk Saysangkhi, a diabetic, was left to die without medication, contact with his relatives or adequate food. Government officials even refused to admit that Thongsouk Saysangkhi had died until several weeks after his death in February 1998.

Prisoners of conscience Feng Sakchittaphong, Latsami Khamphoui and Thongsouk Saysangkhi, all former government officials, were arrested in 1990 after they wrote letters advocating peaceful political and economic change in Laos.

THONGSOUK SAYSANGKHI

Amnesty International has repeatedly called for their immediate release. They were held in pre-trial detention for two years, spending some of that time in dark isolation cells.

In 1992, after unfair trials, they were convicted, sentenced to 14 years' imprisonment and transferred to Prison Camp 7 where they were held in a single prison cell which measured 6m x 6m.

A gap between the bottom of the walls and the concrete floor allowed cold winds to enter the cell. They were made to sit in silence and were only permitted to leave the cell once a fortnight to bathe. They were threatened with beatings if they spoke to each other, and a prison guard was stationed at the door of the cell to enforce this rule. Even now they are held in darkness, except during mealtimes, and are only allowed to bathe once every one or two weeks. Conditions at the prison are so severe that they are recognized as cruel, inhuman or degrading treatment or punishment by the UN Committee against Torture.

Register to take action against torture at www.stoptorture.org

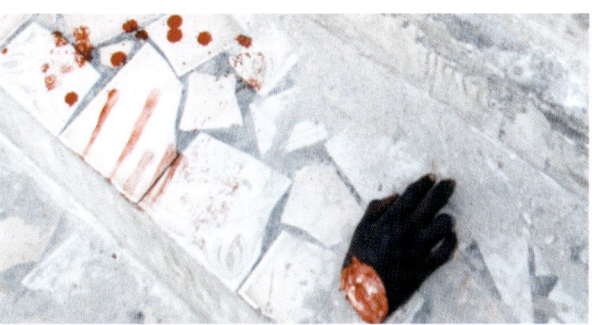

The right hand of a Somali teenager, displayed in the street for all to see. The 19-year-old from Mogadishu was sentenced to amputation of his right hand and left foot by an Islamic court for threatening a woman with a knife and stealing a $1.50 scarf.

cloaked in the respectability of a "legal" punishment.

Judicial corporal punishment takes different forms. Among the most common still in use are amputation, branding and various forms of flogging, including whipping and caning. Some, such as amputation, are deliberately designed to permanently mutilate the human body. However, all of these punishments can cause a range of long-term or permanent injuries.

"...Two prison warders took me to the flogging room... I was shivering and perspiring with fear. Then I heard the cane. A split second later I felt it was tearing across my buttocks. I screamed and struggled like a mad animal... I just could not control my screams. It went on and on, one stroke, one minute. Some prisoners urinate and even faint because of the pain... My buttocks swelled to twice their normal size... The pain burns in your mind long after it is over. Until now I have nightmares about it..."[3]

These are the words of a 40-year-old man recalling the pain, fear and humiliation of being caned in Singapore when he was 17. In some countries victims have been sentenced to hundreds of lashes, resulting in permanent disability or even death.

The victims of amputation, mutilation and branding are not only permanently maimed, they are also stigmatized as criminals for the rest of their lives. In Iraq, for example, following the Gulf War, people convicted of offences including theft and desertion from the army were branded with an "X" mark on the forehead.

Some states defend judicial corporal punishment by claiming that it is a "lawful sanction" and therefore not covered by the international prohibition of torture.[4] However, the term "lawful sanctions" must be understood to mean sanctions which are lawful under both national and international standards. In 1992 the Human Rights Committee, in an authoritative General Comment, stated that the prohibition of torture and ill-treatment under the International Covenant on Civil and Political Rights "must extend to corporal punishment".[5] In a resolution adopted in April 2000, the UN Commission on Human Rights stated that "corporal punishment, including of children, can amount to cruel, inhuman or degrading punishment or even to torture".[6]

Judicial corporal punishments are unlawful because they entail key elements of torture and ill-treatment, including the deliberate infliction of severe pain and suffering as a punishment. Legalizing a practice at national level cannot make something which is contrary to international law "lawful". As stated by the UN Special Rapporteur on torture, "corporal punishment is inconsistent with the prohibition of torture and other cruel, inhuman or degrading treatment or punishment…"[7]

Some proponents of judicial corporal punishment justify it on cultural or religious grounds. But culture is not static and traditions are constantly being reshaped by new realities. Punishments that may have been widely accepted in the past, today appear manifestly cruel and degrading. Local human rights activists are increasingly challenging these practices, using the universality of human rights as their foundation.

Violence in the home and community

Sabira Khan was married in Pakistan at the age of 16 to a man more than twice her age. Shortly after the wedding in 1991 her husband told her that she must never see her family again. In December 1993, when she was three months' pregnant, Sabira tried to see her family. In response to this perceived insubordination, Sabira's husband and his mother poured kerosene over Sabira and set her on fire. She sustained 60 per cent burns but survived, badly scarred. When Sabira tried to gain justice through the courts, she was thwarted. The magistrate in Jhelum upheld her husband's argument that Sabira was insane and had set herself on fire. An appeal is pending before the Rawalpindi High Court bench.

Like many victims of torture, Sabira Khan suffered terrible

pain, deliberately inflicted. Powerless in the hands of her immediate attackers and treated with contempt by the system which should have protected her, she is scarred for life. What distinguishes her ordeal from that of most of the other victims mentioned in this report is that her attackers were not government officials, but members of her own family.

States are responsible for protecting people not only against torture and ill-treatment by their own agents, but also against similar practices by private individuals ("non-state actors"). The state may be accountable in a number of different ways: it is responsible for abuses by private individuals or entities to whom it delegates responsibilities; it shares responsibility for acts of violence by private individuals when it supports or tolerates them; it may also be held responsible when it fails in other ways to provide effective protection against torture or ill-treatment.

AI's recent work on abuses by private individuals has included publications about violence against women in Pakistan,[8] female genital mutilation[9] (a traditional practice which leaves millions of women with serious injuries) and human rights abuses suffered by women trafficked from the former Soviet Union into Israel.[10]

Trafficking in human beings is a worldwide phenomenon. Governments have tended to address trafficking in terms of dealing with organized crime or illegal immigration, rather than in terms of protecting the human rights of the victims. In a report on women and girls who are trafficked from countries of the former Soviet Union to work in Israel's sex industry, AI highlighted the failure of the Israeli government to protect their human rights. Many of the women and girls are subjected to violence, including

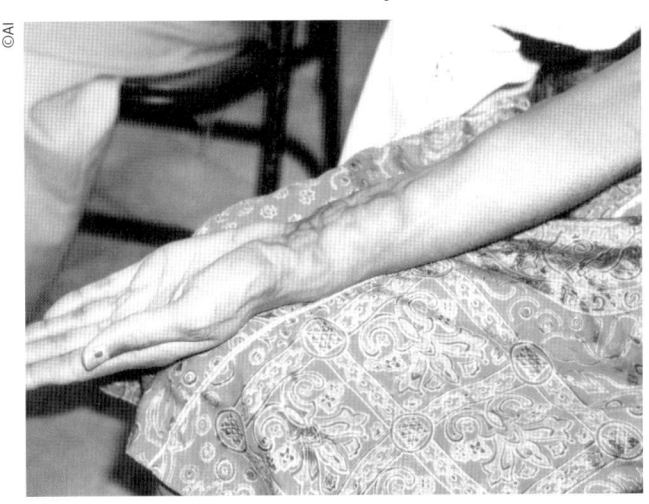

Victim of domestic violence in Hyderabad, February 1999. Women in Pakistan face violent, sometimes lethal, assaults for "shaming" family honour.

Torture by private individuals

The UN Convention against Torture establishes the responsibility of the state for acts of torture inflicted "with the consent or acquiescence of a public official". For example, failure to provide protection against violent racist attacks, may amount to consent or acquiescence in torture.

Under international human rights law, states also have an obligation to act with due diligence to prevent, investigate and punish abuses of human rights, including acts by private individuals. This basic principle of state responsibility is established in all the core human rights treaties. The International Covenant on Civil and Political Rights, for example, obliges states to "ensure" the rights set out in that treaty, including the right to freedom from torture, an obligation which the Human Rights Committee extends to acts inflicted by people acting in a private capacity.[11]

The European Court of Human Rights has also affirmed that under the European Convention on Human Rights, states are required to take measures to ensure that individuals are not subjected to torture or inhuman or degrading treatment or punishment, including such ill-treatment administered by private individuals. In 1998, the Court found that the United Kingdom had violated Article 3 of the Convention (prohibition of torture or ill-treatment) by failing to provide adequate protection to a nine-year-old boy beaten with a cane by his stepfather.[12]

The concept of due diligence is a way to describe the threshold of effort which a state must undertake to fulfil its responsibility to protect individuals from abuses of their rights.[13] A state cannot, for example, avoid responsibility for the ill-treatment of domestic workers by arguing that the abuse took place in the privacy of the employer's home, or that it is justified by social or cultural practices. Due diligence includes taking effective steps to prevent such abuses, to investigate them when they occur, to prosecute the alleged perpetrator and bring them to justice through fair proceedings, and to provide adequate compensation and other forms of redress. It also means ensuring that justice is imparted without discrimination of any kind.

AI considers that acts of violence by private individuals can constitute torture or ill-treatment when they are of the nature and severity envisaged by the concept of torture or cruel, inhuman or degrading treatment or punishment in international standards and when the state has failed to fulfil its obligation to provide effective protection.

rape. They are held captive in apartments, sometimes in wretched conditions, with no passport or money. Yet few of the people responsible are ever brought to justice. In 1998, the Human Rights Committee expressed its regret that "women brought to Israel for the purposes of prostitution... are not protected as victims of trafficking but are likely to bear the penalties of their illegal presence in Israel by deportation."[14]

The spectrum of abuses faced by children in the family and community ranges from ill-treatment in institutions to child abuse in the home, from child trafficking to child bonded labour. Some of these abuses can amount to torture or ill-treatment. The Convention on the Rights of the Child places an obligation on states to protect children not only from torture or ill-treatment by state officials, but from all forms of physical or mental violence or abuse while in the care of "parents, legal guardians or any other person who has the care of the child".

Many children are abused in the care of institutions, such as schools and orphanages, that are supposed to look after them. Often, even when abuses become widely known, the authorities fail to take decisive action to protect the children. Corporal punishment in schools takes place in many countries, despite condemnation by the Committee on the Rights of the Child of the use of corporal punishments in both schools and in the family. Other UN human rights bodies have also stated that protection against torture and ill-treatment extends to educational institutions.

Holding states accountable for abuses by non-state actors is of crucial importance in the struggle to defend the human rights of women, children, racial and sexual minorities, and others facing discrimination. On a daily basis, this discrimination manifests itself through violence, whether in the form of domestic violence, or racist or homophobic hate crimes. Institutionalized discrimination often means that the victims are also less likely to receive protection and support from the authorities. Governments cannot be selective in fulfilling their obligations. They must strive to eradicate torture and ill-treatment for everyone, wherever it occurs and whoever the perpetrator may be.

For the victims of violence, the pain and suffering are as intense, regardless of who the perpetrators are or the manner of the state's failure to protect them. States have a responsibility to prevent, prosecute and ensure redress for these abuses, and AI calls on them to do so.

Torture – a weapon of war

"I was raped by two of them. Then they brought more četniks [Serb nationalist paramilitaries] in who wanted to rape me. I said no. They said that they would throw my child out the window."

"They told me they would like us to give birth to četnik children... They told me, 'we will do everything so that you never even think of returning'."[15]

These women were raped in Foča/Srbinje as part of a systematic campaign of terror during the war which tore the former Yugoslavia apart in the 1990s. The conflict in Foča, a town in the south of Bosnia-Herzegovina, began in April 1992. Bosnian Serb and Yugoslav armed forces took control of the town and surrounding villages and rounded up Bosnian Muslims and Bosnian Croats. Men were taken to a number of detention centres where many "disappeared". Women were held in detention centres, and in places specifically organized for sexual enslavement and rape. Scores of women, children, and the elderly were held in the Partizan Sports Hall, where women were taken out every night to be raped. Women and girls who were injured as a result of sexual abuse or beatings received no medical care. Two women reportedly died there as a result of beatings. Some of those alleged to be responsible have been arrested and brought before the International Criminal Tribunal for the former Yugoslavia.

Most casualties of today's wars are civilians, not soldiers. In modern conflicts, terrorizing civilian populations has become a common means of waging war. This almost invariably involves the use of torture. In Algeria the practice of torture by the security forces had been virtually eradicated in the period from 1989 to

1991, but they started to use it again at the beginning of the current conflict in 1992 and its use quickly became widespread.

At any time in recent years there have been some 30 or more armed conflicts being fought simultaneously in different parts of the world. Most are not wars between states, but internal armed conflicts within one country. These conflicts range from low-intensity guerrilla wars to all-out civil wars between well-equipped armies.

Even in the midst of war, the international prohibition of torture still applies. Armed political groups do not have the same responsibilities as states, since they are not parties to international human rights treaties. However, members of such groups are obliged to respect international humanitarian law, also known as the laws of war. The four Geneva Conventions of 1949 and their two Additional Protocols of 1977 are the main treaties which codify the laws of war. The Geneva Conventions prohibit the use of torture in international armed conflicts against those protected by the Conventions, such as civilians in occupied territory and prisoners of war. Under the Geneva Conventions, torture in an international armed conflict is a "grave breach" of the laws of war — a war crime. Torture and ill-treatment are also prohibited under Article 3 common to all four Geneva Conventions (known as "common

Mobutu military camp, Kinshasa, Zaire (now the Democratic Republic of the Congo), 1997. A soldier holds a gun to the head of a captured member of a Hutu militia member in Rwanda. The protracted and complex conflict in this country has seen torture and other atrocities committed by many of the parties to the conflict.

> According to AI's survey, torture and ill-treatment have been inflicted by state agents in counter-insurgency operations or situations of armed conflict in more than 30 countries since 1997. The survey also found that torture and ill-treatment have been inflicted by armed political groups in more than 30 countries since 1997.

Article 3"), which applies to internal armed conflicts. Common Article 3 of the Geneva Conventions applies not only to governments but to members of armed forces which oppose them. Torture in violation of common Article 3 is recognized as a war crime under the Rome Statute of the International Criminal Court, which was adopted in 1998 but had not yet come into force by October 2000.

Rape of women was reported to be widespread and systematic in parts of the Democratic Republic of the Congo (DRC) occupied by armed political groups in 1999. However, most victims keep silent because they fear rejection by their husbands and social ostracism. Combatants who raped female patients at a hospital in Kindu, DRC, in early 1999, reportedly boasted that they had infected the women they raped with the HIV virus.

In Colombia civilians living in areas disputed by government forces, their allied paramilitaries and armed opposition groups have been the principal victims of political violence including torture. During 1999, at least 1,000 people were victims of politically motivated killings. A further 1,000 were kidnapped by paramilitary organizations and armed opposition groups and held for ransom or political reasons. Many were tortured, often by being mutilated, particularly as a prelude to murder by paramilitary forces. Both government-linked forces and opposition groups have tortured captives.

A group of armed members of the Liberation Tigers of Tamil Eelam (LTTE). The LTTE, which is fighting for an independent Tamil state in the north and east of Sri Lanka, is responsible for abducting, torturing and killing Sinhalese and Muslim civilians.

© Rex Features

TAKE A STEP TO STAMP OUT TORTURE

©Associated Press/Kevin Capon

When British soldiers entered this building in the Kosovan capital Pristina after the 1999 conflict, they claimed to have found weapons for torture, including knives, rubber and wooden batons, baseball bats and brass knuckles.

In Sri Lanka both sides in the protracted civil war between government forces and the Liberation Tigers of Tamil Eelam (LTTE) have inflicted torture. The LTTE has been responsible for hanging captives upside down and beating them, making them inhale chilli fumes, inserting pins under their fingernails and burning them with heated rods. Photographs of Kovinthan Mylvaganam, a prisoner held by the LTTE between 1992 and 1995, show clear signs of burning with heated metal on his genitals, thigh, buttocks and back.

In the confusion and terror of armed conflict, it is sometimes difficult to ascertain which side is responsible for torture and other atrocities. What is clear, however, is that torture remains absolutely prohibited.

2: DISCRIMINATION: FERTILE GROUND FOR TORTURE

Discrimination is an assault on the very notion of human rights. It systematically denies certain people or groups their full human rights just because of who they are or what they believe. It is an attack on the fundamental principle underlying the Universal Declaration of Human Rights: that human rights are everyone's birthright and apply to all without distinction. The right to be free from torture is absolute. It cannot be denied to anyone in any circumstances.

Torture feeds off discrimination. All torture involves the dehumanization of the victim, the severing of all bonds of human sympathy between the torturer and the tortured. This process of dehumanization is made easier if the victim is from a despised social, political or ethnic group. Discrimination paves the way for torture by allowing the victim to be seen not as human but as an object, who can, therefore, be treated inhumanely.

Discrimination against certain groups heightens their vulnerability to torture by state officials in a number of different ways. Discrimination enshrined in law (for example, where the law criminalizes homosexuality or restricts women's fundamental freedoms) can act as a licence to torture. Discriminatory enforcement of laws may also affect both a person's chances of coming into contact with the criminal justice system and their treatment once in its hands. For example, in some countries, black people are often still far more likely than whites to be detained and ill-treated on police "stop and search" patrols.

The victim's identity or status may also affect the nature and consequences of their ill-treatment — for example, children held with adults in custody are particularly vulnerable to rape and sexual violence. Victims from marginalized groups may also have less access to legal remedies. Discrimination reinforces impunity, lessening the likelihood of any official action in cases of torture.

Discrimination also means that certain groups are denied equal protection of the law against violence

Bosnian Muslim women in the Tuzla refugee camp (north east Bosnia). They were among 40 women who were systematically raped by Serb militiamen during the war which ripped the former Yugoslavia apart between 1991 and 1995. They agreed to be photographed so that "the world knows the truth" about the war in Bosnia.

inflicted on them in society at large, such as racist attacks, domestic violence against women and homophobic hate crimes. These violent manifestations of prejudice are often facilitated by official inaction.

Governments are obliged under international human rights standards to tackle discrimination in all its forms.[16] This includes taking essential measures to ensure the right of all to be free from torture and ill-treatment, such as repealing discriminatory legislation which facilitates torture and denies equal access to justice, and providing effective protection against violence in the broader community. It also means ensuring that the laws and institutions of the state address the root causes of discrimination, rather than replicating or fomenting it for political ends.

The following sections focus on specific groups of victims of torture today. They highlight some of the patterns AI has identified in the course of its work and the role that discrimination plays in perpetuating them. Focusing on these groups does not imply that these are the sole or principal victims of torture, or that the experiences suffered by other victims are of less concern. Nor should the categorization disguise the fact that different forms of discrimination are interlinked. The identity of every human being is complex, and cannot be reduced to one sole factor such as race, ethnicity, gender, sexual orientation or class.

The aim is to identify patterns of abuse directed at some of today's victims, the particular contexts in which they are at risk, and the forms of ill-treatment which are in some way specific to them or affect them disproportionately. This analysis helps to identify measures needed to overcome these risks.

Discrimination

"The term 'discrimination'...should be understood to imply any distinction, exclusion, restriction or preference which is based on any ground such as race, colour, sex, language, religion, political or other opinion, national or social origin, property, birth or other status, and which has the purpose of nullifying or impairing the recognition, enjoyment or exercise by all persons, on an equal footing, of all rights and freedoms."

Human Rights Committee, General Comment 18

Racism and torture

"Niggers deserve to be hit first, then asked their name."
Senior police officer speaking to subordinate officers at a training session, Vienna, Austria, August 1999.

The death in detention of South African Black Consciousness leader Steve Biko in 1977 focused world attention on the use of torture as an instrument of *apartheid* – the system of racial domination entrenched in South Africa's legal and political system and condemned universally as a crime against humanity. Although nearly a quarter of a century later the *apartheid* system has ended, institutionalized or endemic racism[17] persists in many countries, including South Africa. Worldwide, one of the clearest manifestations of this phenomenon is the prevalence of a pattern of racially motivated torture and ill-treatment by state officials.

According to AI's research, many if not most of the victims of police brutality in Europe and the USA are black or members of other ethnic minorities. In the Americas, torture and ill-treatment of indigenous people, especially in the context of land rights disputes, is a continuing legacy of centuries of subjugation. Rape, mutilation and other methods of torture have been used as weapons of war in recent conflicts with an ethnic dimension in Africa, Asia and Eastern Europe. Racist ill-treatment is nourished by increasingly xenophobic responses to immigration, discrimination in the criminal justice system, and the resurgence of armed conflicts with an ethnic dimension.

Migration

While globalization has meant the free flow of capital across borders, the human flow of migration has faced ever greater obstacles. Immigrants, migrant workers and asylum-seekers who have left or fled their homes in search of a life with basic dignity and security often encounter racist and xenophobic ill-treatment by officials in the "host" country. Harsh treatment of migrants appears to be an increasingly common component of official immigration policy, particularly in countries where xenophobic sentiment has been inflamed among the wider population.

In Western Europe, a pattern has emerged of foreign nationals dying during deportation, apparently as a result of excessive use of force by police and dangerous methods of restraint, in countries including Austria, Belgium, Germany, Switzerland and the UK.

Asylum-seekers have also been ill-treated in detention. A group of 113 asylum-seekers were rescued from a fishing trawler drifting off the coast of Cyprus in June 1998. Several were beaten by police officers while in custody in August and required hospital treatment. In October, during an attempt to enforce a deportation order on the 40 of them held in Larnaca detention centre, officers from the rapid intervention police force threw tear gas into the cells, forced the asylum-seekers to lie face down on the ground, kicked and stamped on them and hit them with truncheons. In Belgium, Blandine Kaniki, an asylum-seeker from the Democratic Republic of the Congo held in a detention centre, complained that she and other inmates had been physically assaulted by helmeted gendarmes armed with batons and shields in November 1998. She subsequently suffered a miscarriage.

In the Middle East, one of the major destinations of migrant workers is Saudi Arabia. Foreign migrant workers have few legal rights and extremely restricted access to protection and redress through the law. Migrant workers have been detained for prolonged periods and ill-treated simply for visa irregularities. Those accused of more serious criminal offences are at heightened risk of torture, including amputations and flogging, and the death penalty. Female migrant domestic workers are at the mercy of their employers; those subjected to abuses such as beatings or rape have little or no practical means of obtaining redress.[18]

Foreign nationals in custody in Japan are at serious risk of ill-treatment at the hands of the authorities. Foreign workers detained pending deportation after expiry of their visas, and foreign nationals in Japanese jails, have suffered arbitrary punishments, humiliation and beatings. Asylum-seekers have sometimes been detained for long periods in solitary confinement. An Egyptian prisoner suffered a series of assaults in Tokyo Detention Centre and was held in appalling conditions in a punishment cell, just for talking at an inappropriate time. "When you leave Tokyo Detention Centre you are not a human being," he told AI. "If you have a dog in your house you don't treat it like this…"

In *post-apartheid* South Africa, refugees and immigrants, particularly from other African countries, have faced police brutality, hostile comments from government officials, and violent attacks by members of the public who blame them for high rates of crime and unemployment in the country. The national Human Rights Commission and non-governmental organizations have responded with public anti-xenophobia campaigns and litigation on behalf of individual victims of human rights abuses targeted at people of "foreign appearance".

Prejudiced policing

Patterns of policing monitored by AI in many countries suggest that ethnicity and race are seen by some law enforcement officials as indicators of criminality.

In Western Europe, black people and other ethnic minorities are routinely detained on suspicion of offences such as drug dealing or not having identity documents in order. Allegations of racist ill-treatment are rarely investigated effectively. Grace Patrick Akpan, a black Italian medical student, was stopped by police officers for an identity check in Catanzaro, Italy, in February 1996. On informing them that she was an Italian citizen, the officers answered that "a black woman cannot be an Italian citizen", and one announced over the police radio that they were bringing in "a coloured prostitute". She was physically assaulted on the street and in the police station, and required two weeks' hospital treatment on release for cuts, bruises and injuries to her head and chest. In October 1999, almost three years after being committed for trial, the two police officers were found guilty of ill-treatment and given two months' probation.

Violent raids on Romani households or communities by massed police officers have been reported in Bulgaria, Slovakia and Hungary. Police officers in these countries and in Romania are often reported to resort to ill-treatment of Roma to intimidate their communities or to extract confessions. Many Roma victims do not complain about their ill-treatment for fear of reprisals.

Aboriginal people in Australia continue to be imprisoned at disproportionately high rates, despite judicial and other inquiries pointing out serious neglect and official disregard for the particular impact of incarceration on aborigines. An alarming

Hungary

Thirteen-year-old Monika (not her real name) was reportedly dragged out of bed on a Sunday morning, slapped around the face by police officers and taken to the police station in her nightclothes. Police officers insulted her, calling her a "dirty whore", and threatened to kill her. Monika is the youngest of six Romani youngsters who were arrested during a violent police raid on an apartment block in north Budapest on 5 September 1999. Just before midday Hungarian police officers broke into two flats in the 13th district, reportedly without explanation and without producing a warrant. Gradually, the group of friends, who were sleeping in the flats after a party the night before, understood that they were being accused of attacking a pregnant woman, and causing her to miscarry.

FOUR OF THE SIX YOUNG PEOPLE ABUSED BY THE POLICE.

The three boys were beaten and threatened with death. Police officers pushed 16-year-old Sándor (not his real name) and 21-year-old Norbert Batyi to the floor and cuffed their hands behind their backs. Then they beat the prostrate youngsters about the head, shoulders and back with a vipera, a three-part retractable weapon. One officer stood on Sándor's wrists while he was handcuffed and lying on the floor. Another officer held him in an armlock, ramming his head against a metal door in the courtyard. Miklós Drótos, aged 17, was beaten in bed and police officers later trod on his neck while he lay on the ground.

The three girls were subjected to racist and sexist slurs. Police officers slapped Elvira Varga, aged 19, around the face and head, perforating her eardrum, after she denied knowing anything about the attack on the pregnant woman. A policeman slapped 17-year-old Lilla (not her real name) on the face and told her: "A baby died because of you."

At the police station, Sándor's head was rammed against the door of the police station. Sándor and Norbert Batyi were beaten for a further 45 minutes in a corridor in the police station, where they could hear Miklós Drótos screaming. When Sándor told police officers that he was having difficulty breathing and that he felt a sharp pain in his chest, an ambulance was called but the police would not allow the paramedics to take him to hospital.

Police officers who interviewed the three girls subjected them to further verbal abuse. Although officers were told that Monika was only 13 years old, they made no attempt to contact her mother, despite requests. When they discovered that Elvira Varga was 19 years old, they told her: "You are not a juvenile. You can be beaten."

The young people's parents arrived at the police station in the early evening. They were soon joined by representatives of the Roma Civil Rights Foundation, and together they filed a complaint. The six were released without charge from custody at around 9pm.

The Hungarian Minister of the Interior justified the police action, claiming that the police took "coercive measures" because the young Roma behaved aggressively. Yet the youngsters were asleep, dressed only in their nightclothes, when the police arrived in large numbers and heavily armed.

Register to take action against torture at www.stoptorture.org

TAKE A STEP TO STAMP OUT TORTURE

Rodney King being beaten by police.

The Rodney King case set in motion an intense debate into police brutality in the USA. Rodney King and his two passengers were ordered out of their vehicle following a car chase on 3 March 1991. Rodney King was struck twice with an electro-shock taser gun. The video tape showed that he was then subjected to 56 baton blows and kicked and punched by three uniformed officers while 21 other officers stood by. Rodney King sustained multiple injuries, including a broken cheekbone, broken ankle and skull fractures.

In April 1992 four police officers charged in the case were acquitted in a state court. The controversial jury decision sparked off serious rioting in Los Angeles in which more than 50 people died.

However, in April 1993 two of the officers were convicted of federal civil rights charges in the case and sentenced to 30 months' imprisonment.

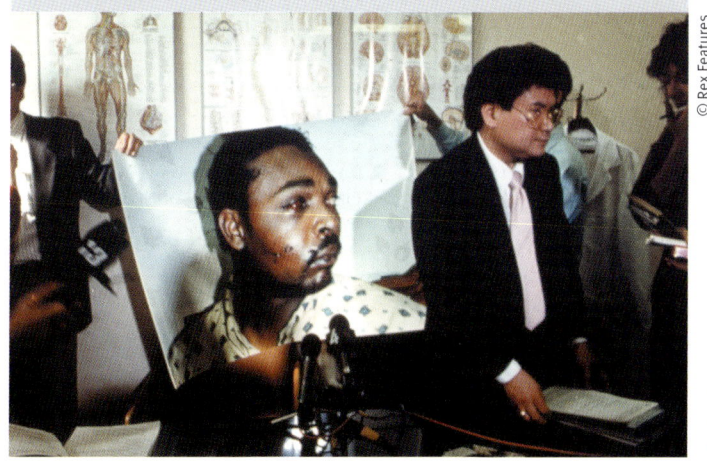

Campaigners expose Rodney King's injuries.

43

number die in custody after claiming they have been ill-treated — many die of illness or commit suicide. Three police officers who were filmed by a security video camera punching and kicking young aborigines in Ipswich, Queensland, in March 1997 were acquitted of assault charges in September 1999 and commended for using violent new restraint techniques.

Torture and ill-treatment at the hands of government forces are part of a much broader pattern of violence inflicted on people for reasons of racism, xenophobia or ethnic hatred. States have an obligation to prevent racial violence by anyone, not just their own officials. The International Convention on the Elimination of All Forms of Racial Discrimination underscores the obligation of states to ensure the right of everyone "to security of person and protection by the State against violence or bodily harm, whether inflicted by government officials or by any individual, group or institution". However, racist attitudes within law enforcement institutions leave victims of racist violence doubly unprotected.

In the UK, the police have been found negligent in their response to racist attacks. An inquiry into the police investigation of the racist killing of black teenager Stephen Lawrence in 1993 found that the investigation had been fundamentally flawed "by a combination of professional incompetence, institutional racism and a failure of leadership by senior officers". In 1999 the Police Complaints Authority found three officers guilty of neglect of duty for failing to carry out a thorough and impartial investigation into the case of Ricky Reel, an Asian student drowned in London in October 1997.

Armed conflict

Many of today's conflicts are drawn along lines of nationalist and ethnic identity, such as the recent wars in the Balkans and continuing fighting in Afghanistan and Central Africa. The political manipulation of perceived ethnic or racial differences fuels many other conflicts raging across the globe.

Russian government forces have cast the net of suspicion over a whole ethnic group in the context of the conflict in Chechnya. Throughout 1999, ethnic Chechens and other people from the Caucasus reported that they were arbitrarily detained, ill-treated and tortured in Moscow and other parts of the Russian Federation.

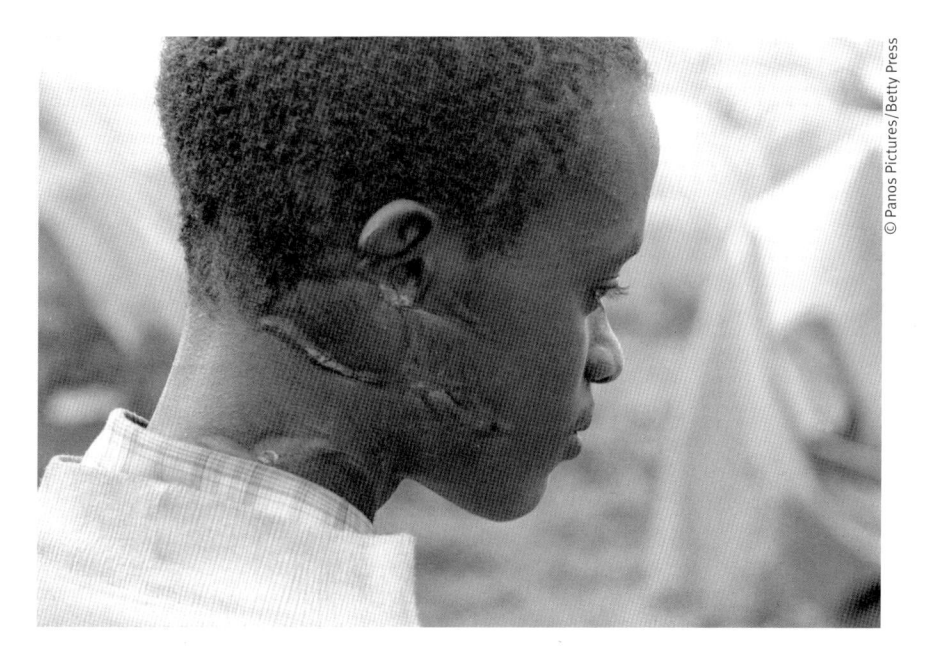

The scars of war. This Tutsi survived a machete wound inflicted during the 1994 genocide in Rwanda.

Within Chechnya itself, Chechen civilians have been raped and subjected to electric shocks and other forms of torture in so-called "filtration" camps. Nobody knows the exact number of detainees held in the "filtration camps", but in early 2000 there were reportedly at least 700 detainees in the Chernokozovo camp alone. A former detainee witnessed a 14-year-old girl being raped by a dozen prison guards in the corridor outside the cells in which he and other detainees were held. The girl had come to visit her detained mother and for the price of 5,000 Roubles she was permitted a five-minute meeting. Her five-minute meeting became a four-day ordeal during which she was locked in a cell, beaten and repeatedly raped by guards.

Largely ignored by the outside world, the conflict in Burundi continues to claim the lives of hundreds of unarmed civilians each year. The continuing struggle for economic and political power has an ethnic dimension and torture is one of the ways in which the Tutsi-dominated armed forces have sought to suppress the insurgency by Hutu-dominated armed opposition groups. Torture and ill-treatment of detainees is rife in Burundi, particularly in police and military custody. People who have been accused of collaboration with armed opposition groups are particularly at risk of torture or of "disappearance". They have been beaten with electric cables and sticks; struck with heavy implements on the joints, the soles of the feet, and the genitals; and tied in excruciatingly painful positions. People from many areas of the country have said that they are afraid to sleep at home because they fear being arrested at night. A 25-year-old refugee interviewed in a camp in Tanzania said he had fled after around 25 young people accused of having links with armed opposition groups were arrested by soldiers in his home area in January 1998. Like many other refugees interviewed by AI, he feared his ethnic origin would lead to him being accused of supporting Hutu-dominated armed opposition groups.

The 2001 UN World Conference on Racism provides a welcome opportunity to cast the spotlight on patterns of racist abuse. The Conference should develop an agenda for action by governments to end torture and ill-treatment.

Torture of women

The last century saw major advances in the struggle for women's human rights. Yet pervasive discrimination means that women are still treated as second class citizens. For all the gains of the last few decades, women are still grossly under-represented in political life, they continue to bear the double burden of work and childcare, to own less and earn less than men and to be denied equal access to education, employment and health care.

Discrimination against women often takes violent forms. Women are raped by armed forces as "spoils of war". They are genitally mutilated in the name of tradition, flogged or killed in the name of honour and terrorized through other forms of domestic violence.

Whether inflicted in custody, in the community or in the home, this violence is intimately linked to women's subordinate position in society. As international standards have recognized, violence against women[19] is both a manifestation of unequal power relations between women and men and a tool of continued subjugation.

Sometimes the perpetrators are state officials. For example, rape is a common instrument of torture in police or army custody.

Bangladeshi prostitutes evicted from a brothel hold a protest rally outside the UN Development Programme office in Dhaka in July 1999. The women alleged that they were tortured by police and hired helpers during the eviction. Members of marginalized groups are particularly vulnerable when they come into contact with security forces.

But much of the violence faced by women in everyday life is at the hands of men known to them as employers, family members or neighbours. Many forms of violence against women in the home and in the community may also constitute torture or ill-treatment. The harm inflicted is often the same or comparable to that which is inflicted on women who are tortured in custody. The purposes may also be similar. The perpetrator may not be a state official, but state inaction is a major factor allowing violence against women to continue. Whatever the context, governments are responsible for protecting and ensuring women's right to be free from torture or cruel, inhuman or degrading treatment.

Violence against women provided by law

Discrimination against women is enshrined in the laws of many countries. In some cases, women who transgress discriminatory laws restricting women's freedom of movement, expression and association are subjected to punishments amounting to torture or cruel, inhuman or degrading treatment.

In mid-June 1999, 24 students having a picnic at their university in Sudan were arrested. They were convicted by the Public Order Court of "committing indecent or immoral acts" and violating strict dress codes, because the female students had been wearing shirts, trousers and T-shirts and because men and women were holding hands during a traditional dance. They were sentenced to up to 40 lashes each and fined.

In Afghanistan, women remain restricted to their homes under Taleban edicts banning them from seeking employment, education, or leaving home unaccompanied by a male relative. Women who defy these edicts are subjected to systematic ill-treatment. Members of the Taleban Ministry for the Propagation of Virtue and the Suppression of Vice have beaten women in the street with long leather truncheons for acts such as allowing their ankles to show, being without a male relative or laughing loudly. (Women have also been tortured and ill-treated for violating social codes restricting women's behaviour in other countries, where such punishments are not provided by law.)

In several countries, judicial corporal punishments amounting to torture may be applied to women convicted of adultery. In some, convictions are based on discriminatory rules of evidence and procedure.

Violence against women in custody

In many countries, rape and other sexual violence are common methods of torture inflicted on women by state officials. Rape or the threat of rape may be inflicted for a number of reasons, such as to extract confessions, or to intimidate, humiliate or punish. Rape always involves the intentional infliction of severe psychological as well as physical suffering. Rape of women detainees by prison, security or military officials is always torture.

The consequences of rape are devastating. In societies where marriage is the only effective means of ensuring women's access to economic resources and securing social acceptance, women who are deemed unfit for marriage as a result of rape may face severe economic hardship and social isolation. In addition to the risk of sexually transmitted diseases including HIV/AIDS, many women must also contend with resulting pregnancy. Women may have less access than men to the resources necessary to pursue a legal case. Many may be deterred from doing so because of social stigma or lack of trust in the willingness of the authorities to investigate complaints.

Two young Kurdish women – 16-year-old high school student N.C.S (full name withheld) and 19-year-old student Fatma Deniz Polattaş – were detained for several days in March 1999 at the Anti-Terror Branch of İskenderun police in Turkey, accused of being members of an armed opposition group. The women were held naked and blindfolded and deprived of sleep, food and access to a toilet. During interrogation, police threatened to rape their parents unless they confessed. N.C.S was hit on the head, genitals, buttocks and breasts, forced to roll naked in water, then suspended and hosed with pressurized cold water. Fatma Deniz Polattaş was punched in the face, breaking a tooth. She was then made to bend over and raped anally with an object she described as "long and serrated". The young women were seen at different times by five doctors, but none reported any signs of torture. Instead the women were subjected to degrading "virginity tests" (examination of the hymen). Although they lodged a complaint, the Iskenderun Chief Public Prosecutor decided not to prosecute the police officers. It was only after an appeal against this decision that in early 2000 a trial was opened against four police officers charged with torture. Complaints of rape by police are rarely investigated in Turkey and very few officers have been convicted. The impunity surrounding rape is compounded by Turkish law, which does not define physical sexual abuse as a crime in the penal code, and defines rape so narrowly (penetration of the vagina by a penis) that it offers no protection in cases such as that of Fatma Deniz Polattaş.

In many parts of the world impunity for rape is reinforced through threats and fear of reprisals. In March 1999 Raja Begum and her daughter Gulsham Bano were among a group of five women detained by Indian soldiers in Jammu and Kashmir, India. Although all five women were reported to have been repeatedly raped, after their release only Gulsham Bano and her mother felt able to lodge a police complaint against the soldiers. The case was reported in the press and prompted public protests. Over the following months, the family was repeatedly threatened and harassed by members of the same army battalion as the alleged torturers. In May 1999 Gulsham Bano and her father were taken into custody. They were released, allegedly on condition that the rape complaint was dropped. The State Human Rights Commission has reportedly taken up the case.

Women are also at risk of torture or ill-treatment in prison. In many countries, the needs of female inmates are grossly neglected, for example where physical restraints are used unnecessarily on sick and pregnant women, posing a serious health threat. In some countries, separate detention or prison facilities for women do not exist, increasing the risk of rape and sexual abuse by other inmates. Failure to provide separate detention facilities may amount to official consent or acquiescence in torture or ill-treatment. Women prisoners who are supervised by male guards, in contravention of international standards, are at particular risk.

Violence against women in armed conflict

Rape of women by combatants in armed conflicts has been a persistent practice for centuries. Mass rape of women from the "enemy" population continues to be a favoured weapon of war. In the recent conflicts in the former Yugoslavia, central Africa, Sierra Leone and elsewhere, rape was part of a cruel and calculated strategy to terrorize whole communities and to force civilians to leave their homes. In Sierra Leone rape continues to be used against unarmed civilians as a tactic of armed conflict.[20] In the words of the UN Special Rapporteur on violence against women, "sexual violence against women is meant to demonstrate victory over the men of the other group who have failed to protect their women. It is a message of castration and emasculation of the enemy group. It is a battle among men fought over the bodies of women."[21]

Women make up the majority of refugees and internally displaced people uprooted by conflict. They are extremely vulnerable to rape and sexual abuse at borders (for example, by guards who demand sex in return for safe passage) and in refugee camps. In West Timor, Indonesia, there were reports of sexual violence against female refugees who had fled the violence in neighbouring East Timor in September 1999. East Timorese women were reported to have been taken at night from refugee camps in West Timor and raped by members of pro-Indonesian militia. Refugees in West Timor said that some women were forced to work as prostitutes while others were held in sexual slavery by militia commanders or Indonesian army officers.

In Guatemala, mass rape of indigenous women was a component of the government's counter-insurgency strategy during the civil war. The official Historical Clarification Commission, set up at the end of the war in 1996 to investigate human rights violations during the conflict, called for psycho-social rehabilitation, including community health care, to help overcome the unresolved traumas suffered by these abused

Sierra Leone. This 38-year-old woman had her arm cut off by rebel forces who attacked her farm in 1997. She is now at the Murray Town camp for amputees in Freetown, where she has been fitted with an artificial arm and is relearning skills such as planting.

women and their communities. Several years later, no such programs had been initiated.

Recent developments in international law have strengthened the legal tools for combating gender-specific forms of torture in armed conflict, whether committed by governments or armed groups. Several judgments of the International Criminal Tribunals for the former Yugoslavia and Rwanda have made an important contribution to ending impunity for violence against women in armed conflict. So has the adoption of the Rome Statute of the International Criminal Court, which gives the Court jurisdiction over the war crimes of rape, sexual slavery, enforced prostitution, forced pregnancy, enforced sterilization and other forms of sexual violence when committed in the context of armed conflict, whether international or internal. It also provides that such conduct may, under defined circumstances, constitute crimes against humanity whether in peacetime or in war.

Violence against women in the community and home

At all stages of their lives, women across the globe are vulnerable to various forms of violence. However different its manifestations, this violence is inflicted solely because they are women or else affects women disproportionately. Assessing the scale of violence against women in the home or in the community is difficult, as it is often under-reported.

In infancy and childhood, girls are at risk of physical, sexual and psychological abuse in such forms as selective malnutrition, denial of equal access to medical care, bonded labour and sexual abuse within the family. It has been estimated that some two million women and girls are subjected every year to genital mutilation, one of many harmful traditional practices rooted in gender-based discrimination.

Many of the most violent forms of gender-based abuse occur within the family. In India, more than 5,000 women are reported to be killed annually by their husbands and in-laws. Many are burned to death in "accidental" fires if their husbands' demands for dowry before and after marriage are not met. In Bangladesh, hundreds of women have been maimed and scarred in acid attacks, for such reasons as rejecting marriage proposals or being unable to meet dowry demands. In several countries, women are attacked or killed with impunity in the name of "upholding family honour", for example when the woman has allegedly committed adultery, has fallen in love with someone of whom the family disapproves or has "brought dishonour" by being raped. For example, Jameela Mandokhel, a 16-year-old mentally retarded girl, was raped in March 1999 in Pakistan. Upon her return to her community in the Kurram Agency, a tribal council decided that she had defiled tribal honour, and had her shot dead. The government took no action.

Violence against women is often driven by economic and social forces which exploit women's labour and the female body. Thousands of women and girls from economically deprived backgrounds are sent abroad to work as domestic workers, where they are at particular risk of physical and sexual abuse by their employers. Thousands more face similar risks when they are trafficked for the purposes of prostitution and sexual slavery.

The ever-present threat of sexual violence – whether in custody, in armed conflict, in the community or in the home – is one of the key factors preventing women from enjoying human rights on an equal basis with men. If rape of women in custody frequently goes unpunished, that impunity extends to rape within the home or the community.

A range of factors compound the difficulties of bringing rapists to justice. Some countries fail to criminalize certain forms of sexual violence (such as marital rape). In others complaints are not registered by police or not pursued with vigour.

Discriminatory laws or attitudes within the criminal justice system can also prevent women from lodging complaints. Discriminatory rules of evidence in Pakistan, for example, mean that a rape victim may herself be prosecuted for adultery or fornication if she makes a complaint but cannot provide four male Muslim witnesses to testify that she did not consent to sexual intercourse.

Prosecutions for rape may be hampered by rules of evidence regarding proof that the women did not consent or by the difficulties of corroboration. Court practice and procedures may exacerbate the complainant's ordeal. Sentences not commensurate with the gravity of the crime send a message that violence against women can be committed with impunity.

In some countries, abuses such as domestic violence and other violence against women are not criminalized in law. Even where such crimes are recognized in law, law enforcement and judicial authorities frequently fail to act with due diligence to prevent and punish such crimes.

International standards set out the steps which governments must take to protect women against violence in the home and in the community and to ensure their right to be free from torture and other ill-treatment.[22] These include putting in place appropriate legislative, administrative and other sanctions to prosecute and punish violence against women, to provide compensation and adequate remedies to the victims, and to put in place effective measures for prevention.

The reinforcement of these standards in recent years is largely thanks to the efforts of women's rights activists across the globe. Such activism can carry great risks.

Pakistani human rights lawyers Hina Jilani and her sister Asma Jahangir[23] have received death threats for their work on violence against women. Hina Jilani narrowly escaped injury in 1999 when one of her clients, Samia Sarwar, who was seeking divorce after years of domestic violence, was shot dead in her office at the instigation of Samia's relatives. Samia Sarwar's death illustrates how much remains to be done to ensure that women are free from torture in all spheres of their lives.

Torture and sexual identity

In Uganda, being lesbian or gay is a crime punishable by life imprisonment. In September 1999 President Yoweri Museveni publicly ordered the police to look for homosexuals, lock them up and charge them. The following month, five people were arrested at a meeting in Kampala by army and police officers. They were accused of being homosexual and held in illegal detention centres, army barracks and police stations for up to two weeks before being released without charge. All five were tortured. One of those arrested said "they tortured me by kicking me on my stomach and slapping my face until it bled. I was made to sleep in a small toilet that was so dirty as it was the only toilet used by all the inmates. The next day I was told to clean the toilet for one week, twice a day, using my bare hands." A number of Ugandans fled the country fearing arrest. In November 1999 President Museveni denied any anti-gay persecution. Homosexuals could live in Uganda, he said, as long as they kept their sexual orientation hidden.

The torture of lesbian, gay, bisexual and transgendered people around the world is concealed behind a veil of secrecy and taboo. It is a worldwide problem – AI has documented numerous cases from every continent – but one that is greatly under-reported.

Protesters call for an end to the harassment of lesbian, gay, bisexual and transgendered people in Chiapas state, Mexico. A pattern has emerged in recent years of violence directed at the gay community in Chiapas.

The stigma surrounding homosexuality in many cultures means that those speaking out are often ignored, further marginalized or abused. While some governments seek to deny that such torture takes place – or even that homosexuals exist in their countries – others openly justify it in the name of morality, religion or ideology. Either way, the effect is that torture goes unchallenged and a sector of the population is left particularly vulnerable.

Discrimination by law

Dozens of countries outlaw homosexuality. Criminalization of homosexuality can lead to non-heterosexuals being arrested and imprisoned simply for having private consensual relationships, meeting friends socially or even "looking gay". Those detained may be tortured or ill-treated to force them to confess to their "crime" or as punishment for it.

The criminalization of homosexuality in Romania has for many years been a fertile ground for torture. In 1992, Ciprian Cucu placed a personal advertisement in a local Romanian newspaper, which was answered by Marian Mutascu. The young men lived together for almost two months, hiding their relationship from family members. Eventually, however, Ciprian Cucu's family reported their relationship to the police. They were arrested in 1993 under penal code provisions prohibiting homosexual relations. Both were tortured in police custody.

Ciprian Cucu recalls:

"I was taken to the pre-trial detention ward... Before I came into the cell, officers told the supervising inmate [delegated by prison guards to maintain order in the cell] that a homosexual was going to be put in the room. As a result, he told me from the very start that I had to have sex with him if I did not want things to go very badly. At first I resisted, but after a few blows, I was forced to give in. It was the first time I was raped – but not the last."[24]

The two were convicted and received suspended prison sentences. Despite international appeals on their behalf, there was no investigation into their torture. Marian Mutascu never recovered from the experience. In 1995, he committed suicide.

In Malaysia, where "sodomy" is a criminal offence, accusations of homosexuality have been used as a pretext to imprison political opponents. Former Deputy Prime Minister Anwar Ibrahim was dismissed and accused of "sodomy" in 1998. He was beaten by police while in incommunicado detention in September 1998. Following widespread protests at this high profile case, a former national police chief was sentenced in March 2000 to two months in prison for the beating. Several close associates of Anwar Ibrahim were forced under torture to "confess" to having had sexual relations with him. Two men who lodged formal complaints about their treatment – which included being stripped naked and forced to simulate the sexual acts they were accused of – were subsequently charged with perjury. Despite testimony that he had been tortured, the confession of one of these men, Sukma Darmawan, was admitted as evidence in the sodomy trial of Anwar Ibrahim. Anwar Ibrahim and Sukma Darmawan were convicted of "sodomy" in August 2000. Anwar Ibrahim was sentenced to nine years in prison. Sukma Darmawan was sentenced to six years' imprisonment and four strokes of the cane.

In other countries too, judicial corporal punishment amounting to torture or ill-treatment is applied by law as a sanction for certain forms of sexual behaviour, including homosexual acts. On 16 April 2000, Associated Press reported that a Saudi Arabian court had sentenced nine young men to prison sentences and up to 2,600

Gay men and lesbians wave rainbow flags during the first ever gay pride parade in Tel Aviv, Israel, in June 1998. Over the last two decades national movements for gay and lesbian rights have emerged all over the globe. They have campaigned for an end to police brutality, the decriminalization of homosexuality and equal protection of the law in the face of homophobic violence and discrimination.

lashes each for "deviant sexual behaviour", apparently because of their sexual identity.

As these examples illustrate, laws criminalizing homosexuality not only deprive a sector of the population of basic human rights, they may also act as a licence to torture or ill-treat those detained. AI campaigns against such laws and considers those imprisoned solely on grounds of sexual orientation to be prisoners of conscience.

Institutionalized prejudice

Torture and ill-treatment is not limited to countries where homosexuality is illegal. Institutionalized prejudice means that lesbians, bisexuals, gay men and transgendered people who come into contact with the law for other reasons may be targeted for abuse, in particular rape and other sexual violence.

Marli Jose da Silva Barbosa and Rosana Lage Ligero, a lesbian couple, were arrested by civil police in Pernambuco, Brazil, in connection with a murder inquiry in June 1996. Both women alleged that they were verbally abused because of their sexual orientation, slapped and beaten with a long strip of rubber cut from a car tyre. The police chief and another officer rubbed their penises in Marli's face while she was handcuffed and threatened to remove her underwear "so that you can learn to be a proper

Argentina

Vanesa Lorena Ledesma was arrested in Córdoba, Argentina, on 11 February 2000. Five days later she was dead. A police report recorded that she had died as a result of a "cardiac arrest". However, an autopsy reportedly revealed that her body showed signs of torture including indications that she had been beaten while handcuffed; severe bruising to the feet, arms, back and shoulders were recorded. There also appeared to be a discrepancy of at least a day between the actual time of death and that recorded by the police responsible for her detention. Complaints about the treatment of Vanesa Lorena Ledesma have been lodged with both the provincial and national authorities.

Vanesa Lorena Ledesma, a 47-year-old transvestite whose legal name was Miguel Angel Ledesma, was an active member of the United Transvestites Association of Córdoba. She was detained in a bar during a fight and charged with damaging the bar. At the police station she was segregated from other prisoners; apparently the reason given for holding her in incommunicado detention was not to protect her, but to avoid other detainees having to share a cell with a "sick" person. According to reports, Vanesa Lorena Ledesma was HIV-positive and attended the local hospital for periodic check-ups which indicated that she was in good health.

Lesbian, gay and transgendered people continue to be the victims of harassment and discrimination at the hands of the Argentine police. Provincial legislation, which allows the police to detain people for acts which are not criminal offences, has frequently been used to detain transvestites, transsexuals, gay men and lesbians. There are concerns that these powers of detention have facilitated torture or ill-treatment.

There are continuing reports that lesbian, gay and transgendered people in Argentina are being detained in police stations in cruel, inhuman and degrading conditions and that they are the victims of beatings, sexual harassment and extortion

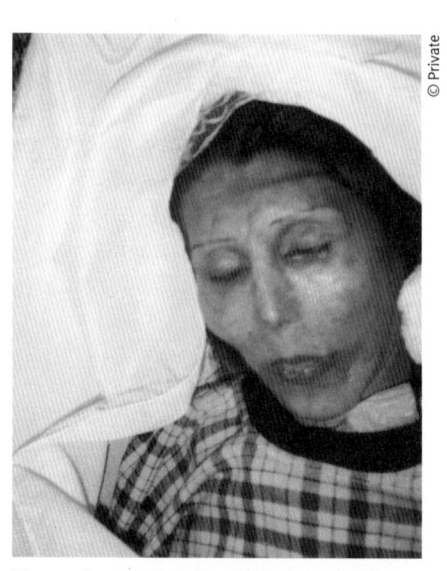

VANESA LORENA LEDESMA AFTER HER DEATH.

by the officers responsible for their detention. Nadia Echazu, a transvestite, was walking in a Buenos Aires street in December 1997 when she was stopped by four men, believed to be police officers. They hit her, pinned her arms behind her back and pushed her to the ground, before forcing her into their car. She was taken to 'Seccional 25' police station where she was kicked and beaten all over her body by police. When she screamed in pain she was put into a straitjacket which was only removed when other detainees protested. That same day Nadia Echazu had been due to appear at a tribunal investigating the treatment of transvestites detained at police stations 23 and 25. Nadia Echazu was released without charge late in the evening.

Many victims have not lodged complaints about their treatment for fear of reprisals. Those complaints which have been lodged have largely been ignored by the authorities or have been investigated in a way which suggests that, despite the gravity of the allegations, they are not being taken seriously.

Register to take action against torture at www.stoptorture.org

woman". Rosana was made to strip by the policemen who had threatened to rape Marli. He pulled her hair and rubbed his penis in her face. Once in prison, their injuries were noted by staff but the women refused a medical examination as it would have meant being escorted by the policemen who had tortured them. Despite a national campaign for the torture allegations to be fully investigated, no action has been taken to date against the policemen involved.

Lesbian, gay, bisexual and transgendered people in prison often find themselves on the lowest rung in the prison hierarchy. In Jamaica, 16 prisoners were killed and 40 injured in anti-gay attacks at St Catherine's District Prison and Kingston's General Penitentiary in August 1997. The disturbances started after the Commissioner of Corrections announced his intention to distribute condoms to guards and prisoners in an effort to control the spread of HIV/AIDS. Guards walked out in protest at the insinuation that they were having homosexual relations with inmates (same sex relations are illegal in Jamaica). Inmates went on the rampage, targeting prisoners thought to be gay. No action is known to have been taken against the prison authorities.

A group of transvestites protest outside the central police station about the death in custody of Vanesa Lorena Ledesma.

Torture and ill-treatment are not limited to prison or police custody. Ill-treatment may also occur during raids on bars or other public meeting places. Rebecca Sevilla, a human rights defender from Peru, recalls a raid on bars and clubs in Lima in 1994: "…a very violent raid was carried out in the capital where about 75 lesbian women were beaten up and ill-treated by the police. Prostitutes get a very rough time in jail. But the treatment of lesbians was even worse. Lesbians were beaten up because however degrading prostitution can be, it is still regarded as normal behaviour, whereas lesbianism is seen as too threatening to the status quo." More recent sweeps by Peruvian police on gay and lesbian bars in Lima have also resulted in beatings and homophobic verbal abuse.

Ill-treatment may also occur in the context of street demonstrations. In the USA, New York police officers reportedly ill-treated peaceful demonstrators attending a rally organized by lesbian and gay rights activists in October 1998. Formal complaints were lodged relating to 70 incidents during and after the demonstration, including physical abuse of demonstrators and homophobic insults. The rally itself was in protest at the murder of Matthew Shepard, a student viciously battered to death in Wyoming in 1998 because he was gay. The case brought to international attention the spectrum of violence inflicted on people worldwide because of their sexual orientation or identity.

In the absence of effective protection and remedies against torture and other violations, many lesbian, gay, bisexual and transgendered people are forced to flee their country in search of physical safety. Since 1992, when an Argentine gay man was granted asylum in Canada on the grounds that he had been tortured by police because of his sexual orientation, a growing number of countries have accepted asylum claims on this basis. However, many asylum-seekers find it difficult to provide supporting evidence for their claim because patterns of persecution based on sexual orientation in their country are insufficiently documented by human rights organizations and other trusted sources. Others are afraid to speak openly to the immigration authorities about their sexual orientation. For example, F.C., a Honduran claiming asylum in the USA, omitted key details of the homophobic ill-treatment he was fleeing because he feared that fellow inmates in the immigration detention centre would turn violent if he disclosed his sexual orientation. His claim was rejected.

Human rights defenders

Over the last two decades, national movements for lesbian and gay rights have emerged all over the globe. They have campaigned for an end to police brutality, the decriminalization of homosexuality and equal protection of the law in the face of homophobic violence and discrimination. However, this surge of activism in recent years has met renewed attacks on human rights defenders.

In Zimbabwe, members of the human rights group Gays and Lesbians of Zimbabwe have been threatened and denied police protection against attacks by pro-government groups. Meanwhile, President Mugabe of Zimbabwe has maintained his campaign of hate speech against lesbians and gay men, whom he has publicly branded "less than human" and "worse than pigs".

In Brazil, a neo-fascist group calling itself the *Frente Anti-Caus* (FAC), Anti-Chaos Front, planted a bomb in AI's São Paulo office in October 1999. With it was a letter featuring a crude swastika, attacking AI for its work in defence of lesbians, gay men and black people. Eduardo Bernardes da Silva, who worked in the São Paulo office, has since received repeated death threats from the group. In early 2000, the human rights organization *Grupo Tortura Nunca Mais* (No More Torture Group) received letters from the FAC threatening AI, human rights activists, gay men, lesbians and shanty-town dwellers. The letters implied that the group had access to confidential police information. Police investigations into the threats and attacks have made little progress to date.

An AI member at the Pride celebration in Paris, France, in 1997 holds a poster drawing attention to human rights abuses against gays and lesbians including police brutality.

The dangers facing lesbian and gay rights defenders have been recognized by the UN High Commissioner for Human Rights:

> "We must acknowledge that some human rights defenders are even more at risk because of the nature of the rights that they are seeking to protect, particularly when they relate to issues of sexuality, in particular sexual orientation, and reproductive rights."
> **Mary Robinson address to UN General Assembly, Beijing +5 conference, June 2000**

In this campaign, AI aims to lift the veil on torture and ill-treatment based on sexual identity and to help raise awareness about what needs to be done to better protect the rights of lesbian, gay, bisexual and transgendered people.

Torture of children

In March 1997, three boys between the ages of 10 and 12 were arrested while collecting scrap metal from a rubbish dump in Istanbul, Turkey. Accused of stealing a tape recorder, they were taken to Küçükçekmece Police Station and held incommunicado for 32 hours. The boys said they were stripped to their underwear and locked in a toilet, where officers urinated on them and made them lie on human excrement. In order to force them to confess to the theft, the children were asked to "choose" between electric shocks or beating, and were then subjected to both. They were also sexually assaulted. Hospital medical certificates described injuries consistent with their allegations, including large bruises and electricity burns.

Children are entitled to special protection against torture and ill-treatment. Their youth and inexperience renders them particularly vulnerable, and certain forms of treatment – such as solitary confinement – may have a more severe impact on a child than on an adult. Additional safeguards are therefore needed – and are provided in a range of international standards[25] – to protect children.

But youth is no protection against torture: since 1997, children have reportedly been tortured or ill-treated by state officials in more than 50 countries around the world.

In many cases children are ill-treated because their needs are

Punishment cell in a juvenile detention centre, UK. The use of solitary confinement as a disciplinary measure for juveniles is prohibited by the UN Rules for the Protection of Juveniles Deprived of their Liberty.

overlooked in a criminal justice system organized by and for adults. In others, children appear to be deliberately targeted because of their age or dependence. Children are tortured to coerce or punish their parents. Children on the streets may be seen as expendable; those in custody as easy prey for abuse. In armed conflicts, children of an enemy group are often abused precisely because they represent that group's future.

Children in contact with the law

Children forced to live on the streets are particularly vulnerable to arbitrary arrest and ill-treatment. Many survive on begging, petty crime or prostitution — activities which bring them to the attention of the police. Street children sometimes fall victim to "social cleansing" campaigns, in which local business owners pay to have them chased away, attacked or even killed. Others are detained and ill-treated under laws which make destitution, vagrancy and begging criminal offences.

One night in February 1999, a uniformed member of the Guatemalan National Police kicked awake two 15-year-old street children, Lorena Carmen Hernandez Carranza and Nery Mateo Hernandez, in a park in Guatemala City. He accused them of having mugged and knifed someone. As he searched them for weapons, he threw them both to the ground and told them to take off their clothes. He sexually abused Lorena, then left, saying that he would return. The two lodged formal complaints with the assistance of a non-governmental organization (NGO), *Casa Alianza*, but by mid-2000 the officer had not been prosecuted.

Children in police custody are particularly vulnerable to rape and sexual abuse, both by police officers and other detainees.

N.J. [full name withheld], an 11-year-old girl, living in a camp for internally displaced people outside Khartoum, Sudan, was detained in May 1999 by four police officers who mistook her for a vagrant child. She was taken to a police station where one officer reportedly undressed her by

A young prisoner in a juvenile detention facility in Jakarta, Indonesia.

© Tina Gue/Panos Pictures

force and raped her in front of the other three. He then took her to hospital, claiming that she had been found lying outdoors suffering from malaria and meningitis. The doctors treated her for malaria for five days before discovering that she had been raped. Proceedings against the officers were initiated but appear to have stalled.

The specific needs of girls in custody are rarely taken into consideration. The authorities in some countries have argued that the number of young female offenders is comparatively low, and does not justify the provision of dedicated custodial facilities. As a result girls are often detained far from their families and held together with boys or adults, putting them at further risk.

In many countries, the treatment of children held in juvenile detention centres poses a serious risk to their health and well-being. In the USA, staff in juvenile facilities have punched, kicked, shackled, and used chemical sprays and electro-shock devices against children in their care. A Department of Justice investigation in Kentucky, for instance, found that staff in one county detention centre regularly used stun guns and pepper spray to control uncooperative teenagers and to break up fights. Children detained at the facility also reported that they were hit by staff.

Severe overcrowding in the juvenile detention system in São Paulo, Brazil, led to a spate of riots in September 1999. Television scenes of hooded warders beating boys, and riot police firing rubber bullets at anxious relatives waiting outside for news, sparked a public outcry. After years of neglect, conditions in detention centres for young offenders are appalling. Boys sleep on filthy mattresses on concrete floors, two to three boys per mattress. The cells are so overcrowded that many have to sleep sitting up. Because boys are not permitted to go to the toilet during the night, mattresses are soiled with urine, and most boys suffer from skin problems. Boys report regular attacks by warders, including nightly beatings with sticks and iron bars.

Children in armed conflict

Torture is often used to punish and to intimidate the civilian population during armed conflicts. Many children have been tortured because they happen to live in a war zone, because they belong to a targeted group or because of their own or their family's activities. Moreover, children living through armed conflicts are often traumatized by witnessing death and destruction.

Children detained because they or their relatives were suspected of involvement with armed opposition groups have been tortured to elicit confessions or other information. Children were among the hundreds of detainees held at the Khiam detention centre in Israeli-occupied southern Lebanon, run by the South Lebanon Army (SLA) in cooperation with the Israel Defence Force, until its closure in 2000. Held without charge and denied contact

Girls in Uganda receive counselling after they were kidnapped by the Lord's Resistance Army (LRA), 1997.

with lawyers, detainees were routinely tortured and ill-treated. Fatima Ja'afar, aged 16, was detained overnight in October 1999 at the SLA's No.17 Detention Centre. During interrogation she was struck on the head; the next day she was hospitalized with multiple fractures of the skull and memory loss. Following her release the SLA reportedly arrested her parents and detained them overnight.

In Manipur state in India, children, especially boys, are targeted by soldiers who believe them to be supporters or future members of armed opposition groups. Under the Armed Forces Special Powers Act, the security forces enjoy virtual immunity from prosecution for abuses. In February 1998, soldiers arrested 15-year-old student Yumlembam Sanamacha along with two other boys and drove them away in an army jeep. The other two boys,

Sierra Leone

Mabinti [not her real name], now aged 16, was abducted, repeatedly gang-raped and made pregnant by rebel forces. Her ordeal started after rebels attacked the village of Mamamah while retreating from the capital, Freetown, in January 1999. Her parents were killed in the raid and Mabinti was taken by the rebels, first to Lunsar and then to Makeni in Northern Province. "A number of the rebels gang-raped me many times. If I resisted rape, I was denied food and beaten. I was eventually forced to become the "wife" of one of the rebels – the same thing happened to many other girls." When she became pregnant, Mabinti was taken back to her village and abandoned. Not long after, in May 2000, her village was again attacked by rebel forces and she was forced to flee with her grandmother. They walked 40 kilometres before reaching an internally displaced people's camp.

A YOUNG GIRL WHOSE HAND WAS AMPUTATED BY REBEL FORCES IN FREETOWN IN JANUARY 1999.

Murder, abduction, mutilation and rape have been used systematically in a campaign of atrocities carried out by rebel forces against civilians during nine years of internal armed conflict. Groups aligned with the government and government forces have also carried out atrocities. The scale of rape and other forms of sexual abuse has been unprecedented: more than 90 per cent of women and girls abducted by rebel forces during the conflict are believed to have been raped. When rebel forces attacked Freetown in January 1999, more than 4,000 children were reported missing; a year later 2,000 of them, mostly girls, remained missing and were believed to have been abducted. Thousands of people were killed and hundreds of others maimed by having limbs deliberately cut off.

A peace agreement between the government and the rebel Revolutionary United Front (RUF) was signed in July 1999, and initially reduced the scale of abuses. The agreement, however, provided a blanket amnesty for crimes committed during the conflict between 1991 and July 1999 – including the rape of thousands of girls and women, the deliberate killing and mutilation of thousands of men, women and children, and countless other gross abuses of human rights. Large numbers of civilians who should have been released under the terms of the agreement remained held.

The previous pattern of abuses against civilians was quick to re-emerge: since October 1999 killings, mutilations, rapes and abductions by rebel forces have continued to be frequently reported. The capture of some 500 United Nations peace-keepers by rebel forces in early May 2000 and a subsequent resumption of hostilities has increased still further the threat to civilians of human rights abuses.

The amnesty provided by the peace agreement does not apply to abuses since July 1999, yet they continue to be committed with impunity.

Register to take action against torture at www.stoptorture.org

who were released the next day, testified that they saw Yumlembam Sanamacha being tortured by army personnel on their way to a nearby army camp. Yumlembam Sanamacha has not been seen since and the army has attempted to block independent investigations into his "disappearance".

Children are also exploited as combatants by both armed forces and armed opposition groups. More than 300,000 child soldiers are currently being used in conflicts in over 30 countries. Many of these children are abducted and forced to join through torture, brutal ill-treatment and intimidation, including threats against them and their families.

In northern Uganda, thousands of boys and girls have been abducted by the Lord's Resistance Army (LRA), and forced to fight the Ugandan army. The children are subjected to a violent regime. LRA commanders force children to take part in killing others soon after they are seized, apparently to break down their resistance, destroy taboos about killing and implicate them in criminal acts. Abducted children are owned by LRA commanders, with girls allocated to commanders in forced marriages and effectively held as sexual slaves. All children are sent to fight. One 15-year-old girl told AI: "Please do your best to tell the world what is happening to us, the children. So that other children don't have to pass through this violence." Before she managed to escape, she had been forced to kill a boy and she had watched as another boy was hacked to death. Those who have escaped the LRA face an immense struggle to rebuild shattered lives. The medical and social consequences are particularly bad for girls, almost all of whom are suffering from sexually transmitted diseases.

The recently adopted Optional Protocol to the Convention on the Rights of the Child sets 18 as the minimum age for recruitment into armed forces and participation in hostilities. AI opposes the use of child soldiers under the age of 18 and calls on states to ratify and implement this new treaty.

WE
ILL NOT
TOLERATE
UMAN
INJUSTI
OR
MACOU
DRESSED IN
STOP
POLICE
BRUTAL
JUSTICE
FOR
LOUIMA,
CEDEANO
AN M
444
HUMAN

3: IMPUNITY

"He said if I ever talked to anyone about what happened to me, he['d] kill me and everyone in my family."
Extract from the testimony given by Abner Louima at the trial of Officer Justin Volpe

In May 1999, Abner Louima, a Haitian immigrant living in the USA, took the witness stand in a New York federal district court and described how he was tortured in a Brooklyn police station. He had been arrested by New York Police Department (NYPD) officers in August 1997 following a brawl outside a nightclub. In the police station, he was taken in handcuffs to the toilets where he was punched, thrown to the floor and held down as one officer, Justin Volpe, rammed a broken broom stick into his rectum. As he lay howling with pain, Officer Volpe thrust the stick into his mouth. Abner Louima suffered severe internal injuries including a perforated colon and a ruptured bladder, and spent two months in hospital.

This is one of the many cases of police brutality in the USA which AI has documented in recent years. In many ways Abner Louima's case is typical: the victim was a black man arrested following a minor incident whose treatment appears to have been racially motivated.

However, one aspect of the case which marks it out from most others is that the officers responsible were eventually brought to justice. Complaints of police brutality by the NYPD rarely result in criminal convictions and at first Abner Louima's complaint against the officers who tortured him seemed equally doomed. Officers denied the charges, claiming that Abner Louima's injuries had been caused by sex with another man. They wove an elaborate tapestry of lies to cover up their involvement. As in many cases of torture or ill-treatment, the only direct witnesses were other police officers. All over the world, the refusal of officers to give evidence against fellow officers has proved a formidable barrier to bringing those responsible to justice.

However, a rare breakthrough in mid-1999 opened a crack in the wall of impunity. One by one, several police

Protesters demand justice for Abner Louima, a Haitian immigrant who suffered severe internal injuries after New York police officers tortured him at a Brooklyn police station in August 1997. Members of racial and ethnic minorities are disproportionately victimized by US police in many areas, and black officers themselves have complained of the stereotyping of black men as criminal suspects.

officers who had also been at the station that night came forward to testify against the accused. It was only under pressure from federal and departmental investigators that they finally broke the "code of silence" which so often enables police officers to evade accountability.

Shortly after fellow officers gave their testimony – including eyewitness accounts of Officer Volpe brandishing a broomstick soiled with faeces and bragging about his actions – Justin Volpe changed his plea and conceded his guilt. In December 1999 he was sentenced to 30 years' imprisonment. Three other officers were convicted in March 2000 of conspiring to cover up the incident. Another three were charged with making false statements.

Campaigners seeking justice for Abner Louima point to a second crucial element in securing the convictions: the existence of well-documented proof of his severe injuries. Medical evidence helped to corroborate his torture allegations and to refute the explanations advanced by the defence.

A third factor – without which Louima's torturers may never have been brought to justice – was the public outrage and mobilization that the case provoked. Anti-racist campaigners and other human rights activists were joined by thousands of local residents in a series of demonstrations against police brutality. Unusually, New York mayor Rudolph Giuliani, whose hardline anti-crime drive was criticized by campaigners as having encouraged police ill-treatment, also spoke out against the "reprehensible" assault on Louima, calling for "the severest penalties" for those found responsible.

"The sentence today, I hope, will send a clear message that no one is above the law."
Abner Louima at the sentencing of Justin Volpe in December 1999

Impunity – a worldwide problem

In many countries, impunity for torturers – the failure to bring those responsible for torture to justice – is endemic. As Abner Louima's case shows, it usually takes a combination of extraordinary circumstances for a successful prosecution to be brought against a suspected torturer. Whether justice is done may depend on the degree of media interest or public outrage, the incontrovertible nature of the evidence and the capacity of the judiciary to pursue investigations independently and thoroughly. For all too many torture survivors, however, what they experience after the actual torture is over is not justice but further abuse and intimidation.

Torture is one of the most secret of human rights violations. It is normally carried out in places shielded from public scrutiny and considerable efforts are often made to conceal evidence vital to the successful prosecution and conviction of the torturer. Investigations — where they occur — are often stalled because of the inaction, ineffectiveness or complicity of the investigating body.

Even where complaints of torture are pursued, only a tiny proportion of officers prosecuted are eventually convicted. For example, in Turkey, according to official figures, investigations of 577 security officials accused of torture between 1995 and 1999 resulted in only 10 convictions. The UN Committee against Torture found that in Mexico, where torture is widespread, there had been "only two convictions based on the Federal Act to Prevent and Punish Torture and five for homicide resulting from torture" between June 1990 and May 1996.

The stark reality is that most victims of torture around the world are routinely denied justice. Such a chronic lack of accountability creates a climate where would-be perpetrators can continue to resort to torture and ill-treatment, safe in the knowledge that they will never face arrest, prosecution or punishment.

Impunity sends the message to torturers that they will get away with it. Bringing the culprits to justice not only deters them from repeating their crimes, it also makes clear to others that torture and ill-treatment will not be tolerated. However, when the institutions responsible for upholding the law routinely flout it when dealing with their own members, they undermine the whole criminal justice system. Combating impunity means striking at the very heart of this institutional corruption.

Impunity must also be overcome because it denies justice to the victims, robbing them a second time of their rights. Impunity itself can be seen as a multiple human rights violation, denying the victims and their relatives the right to have the truth established and acknowledged, the right to see justice done and

India

Angammal and Guruviah were arrested in July 1998 on suspicion of receiving stolen property. Police arrived at the couple's home in the Madurai district of Tamil Nadu in the early hours of the morning and found Angammal alone. They took her to the local police station and then to Oormechikulam police station, where she was made to spend the night with her hands tied behind her back. Guruviah was arrested the following morning. Both denied any knowledge of receiving the stolen property.

Their interrogation began on 28 July. Police officers tied the couple's hands behind their backs, made them face the wall, and beat them on their backs and buttocks with *lathis* (long wooden sticks).

The couple were transferred to yet another police station, where they were ordered to undress. They were led outside on a chain and beaten until Guruviah lost consciousness.

Back inside the police station, the couple were suspended from the roof of the building and beaten. When Angammal was taken down, she was thrown on the floor, still naked. Guruviah was told that Angammal would be "spoilt" in front of him, unless he confessed and revealed where the stolen jewellery was hidden. Angammal's breasts were bitten and she was kicked in the genitals. When Guruviah was taken down from the roof, the couple were made to simulate intercourse in front of several police officers.

Guruviah was taken to another police station, where police officers beat him, threw chilli powder in his eyes and pierced his fingernails, toenails and tongue with needles.

On 2 August 1998 the couple were taken to the Deputy Superintendent of Police. He was so shocked at their condition that he ordered their immediate admission to a private nursing home. Guruviah died of his injuries later that evening. Angammal was transferred the next day to a government hospital, where she remained for two weeks.

More than two years after her arrest Angammal continues to suffer mental and physical pain as a result of what happened in detention.

Angammal is still pursuing her case through the courts, trying to secure the prosecution of the police officers responsible for her husband's death. Several petitions are pending before the Tamil Nadu High Court, including a request that the investigation be taken out of the hands of the local police and transferred to the Crime Branch of the Criminal Investigation Department. Although Angammal has made a complaint to the State Human Rights Commission, the Commission has so far failed to respond.

Several attempts have been made to silence Angammal and to stop her from publicizing the case. In August 1998 she was offered Rs400,000 (US$9,000) if she agreed not to speak to the Executive Magistrate who was conducting an inquiry into her husband's death. She refused the offer and made a full statement. In January 1999 Angammal was awarded Rs200,000 (US$4,600) from the Tamil Nadu state government as compensation for Guruviah's death.

Register to take action against torture at www.stoptorture.org

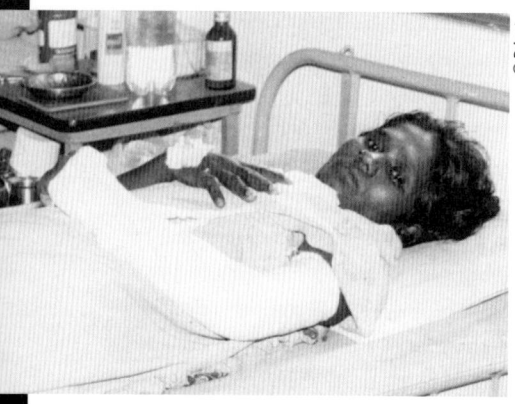

ANGAMMAL

the right to an effective remedy and to reparation. It prolongs the original hurt by seeking to deny that it ever took place – a further affront to the dignity and humanity of the victim.

Past efforts by the international community have been successful in exposing torture and strengthening legal protections against it. The UN Convention against Torture sets out the obligation of states to investigate the facts, bring to justice and punish those responsible, and provide reparation to the victim – all measures which are vital to the struggle to end impunity. It is increasingly accepted that this obligation is a rule of customary international law, which exists regardless of whether a state has ratified the Convention.

However, it is a rule obeyed only exceptionally. Its existence on paper is of little consolation to the many thousands of people who have been tortured with impunity since the Convention was adopted. The fight against torture today must focus on transforming this principle into practice.

Obstacles to justice

Impunity manifests itself in many different forms. In order to take effective action against it, the various factors that give rise to it need to be identified. These vary from country to country. Impunity can arise at any stage before, during or after a judicial process. Mechanisms of impunity may even come into play before an act of torture has been committed. Some typical sources of impunity are explored below.

Evidence is covered up: Unlawful detention practices – such as officers failing to identify themselves or to register detainees, keeping detainees blindfolded or in secret detention, or denying them access to lawyers, relatives or doctors – facilitate impunity by covering over the trail leading from the crime to the perpetrator. Torturers may choose methods which leave few physical traces such as hooding or psychological torture. Officials who have committed torture may subsequently attempt to cover up their crimes by concealing the evidence. For example, medical evidence may be suppressed and medical officers encouraged to falsify reports, while those who carry out their tasks scrupulously may be harassed or even prosecuted.

Victims are denied access to remedies: Sometimes the already terrified victim is intimidated into keeping silent about what happened. Those who do present a complaint may be threatened, attacked or prosecuted on criminal counter-charges such as defamation. Victims from poor and marginalized sectors of the community are often unable to call on the support of lawyers or non-governmental organizations (NGOs), and may be unaware of the legal remedies available to them. In some cases, the law offers only extremely limited remedies as, for example, in situations where individuals cannot bring civil actions or enforce judgments in such actions, or seek criminal proceedings against the alleged torturer.

Investigations are ineffective: In some cases, investigations into torture are carried out by the very organization whose members were responsible for the abuse. Justice can also be thwarted by placing torture investigations under the jurisdiction of military courts which lack independence and impartiality. All too frequently, independent prosecutors or judicial officials fail to act thoroughly and diligently in following up allegations. In some cases they do not have power to act on their own initiative or are unable to constrain the actions of the security forces. Political interference in the judicial process may also result in a decision not to prosecute an alleged torturer. In some cases other institutions with a responsibility for ensuring that justice is done, such as ombudsperson's offices and national human rights commissions, have not been given sufficient powers or resources to be truly effective in combating impunity.

In Mexico, for example, the Attorney General's Office has the contradictory role of investigating alleged human rights violations while employing many of those accused of such violations. The Inter-American Commission on Human Rights has called on the government to strengthen the Office's autonomy and independence.

Complicity of fellow officers: The "code of silence" which operates in many police forces may dissuade officers from giving vital evidence against colleagues accused of torture. The result can be the most blatant injustice. For example, in April 1999 the Supreme Court of Spain severely criticized the fact that it was forced to confirm the acquittal of three national police officers charged with raping and beating a Brazilian woman in 1995. Rita Margarete R., a travel agent, was arrested late one night in Bilbao as she was waiting for a taxi — police apparently assumed she was a sex worker. The provincial court accepted that she had been raped but acquitted the officers because of lack of evidence — no officers had been willing to give evidence against those involved. The Supreme Court was reported as saying that it was incompatible with the democratic rule of law that an "extremely serious and proven case of rape" should remain unpunished because of "archaic corporativist ideas or false camaraderie".

The legal framework for punishing torture is inadequate: In some jurisdictions, domestic law does not prohibit torture in line with the UN Convention against Torture or other relevant international standards. The specific crime of torture may not exist and crimes such as "assault" may have a lesser sanction. Where the crime of torture is established in law, it may be defined or interpreted too narrowly. For example, in China, the crimes of "using torture to coerce a confession", "extorting testimony by violence" and "ill-treating prisoners" are only applicable to a limited range of officials in certain circumstances, and exclude many other acts of torture or ill-treatment covered by the Convention. In May 2000, the UN Committee against Torture echoed AI's call for a revision of the criminal law in China.

There are many other flaws in the legal framework of certain countries which can contribute to impunity. The accused may escape conviction by pleading that they were only following orders, even though this ground is expressly prohibited as a defence in the UN Convention against Torture. The superior officers responsible for ordering or condoning an act of torture may not be held criminally liable. Even where adequate legislation exists, officers who torture may still be charged with lesser offences or the charges may not cover the full range of crimes committed.

In some cases, courts fail to convict despite the existence of convincing evidence which would establish the suspect's guilt beyond reasonable doubt. Even where a conviction is secured, impunity is guaranteed if the sentence is grossly disproportionate to the gravity of the crime.

Judicial rulings are flouted: In some countries, the political authorities regularly ignore rulings by the judiciary, undermining the rule of law and feeding impunity. The Palestinian Authority,

Israel/Occupied Territories

> "On three occasions, while I was on the ground [one of my interrogators] grabbed the shackles on my legs and dragged me along the floor. [Another interrogator] kneed me, breaking one of my ribs"
>
> 'Omar Ghanimat

> "... the methods used... complied with the approved interrogation... procedures"
>
> Department for the Investigation of Police Misconduct

'Omar Ghanimat, a Palestinian, was told by his Israeli interrogators that he would leave the detention centre "crazy or paralysed". He spent the first 48 hours of his interrogation hooded, in *shabeh* (see illustration). Over the weeks that followed he was often forced to hold excruciatingly painful positions. For example, he was forced to squat on his toes in *gambaz*, the "frog" position, for long periods. His interrogators shackled his hands so tightly that the blood supply to his fingers was cut off. They exposed him to extremely loud music and cold temperatures, and routinely deprived him of sleep.

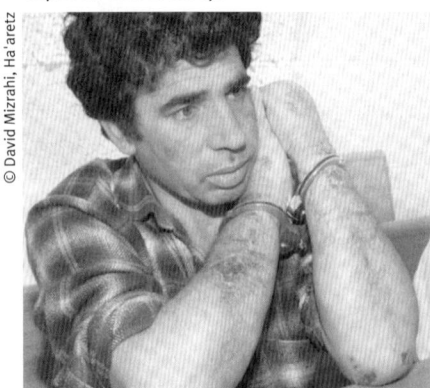

DRAWING SHOWING THE TORTURE METHOD KNOWN AS *SHABEH*.

'OMAR GHANIMAT

Despite permanent damage to 'Omar Ghanimat's health, the Israeli authorities concluded that his treatment had not deviated from authorized procedures.

'Omar Ghanimat was arrested at his home in Surif, Hebron, on 10 April 1997 by Israeli soldiers and members of the Israeli General Security Service (GSS). He was taken to the Jerusalem police district headquarters, where he was repeatedly interrogated by GSS officers and accused of belonging to '*Izz al-Din al-Qassam*, an armed wing of the Islamist group *Hamas* which opposes the peace process with Israel.

Allegra Pacheco, 'Omar Ghanimat's lawyer, made her first visit to the police headquarters in late May 1997. She immediately submitted a petition to the High Court to stop the use of torture. 'Omar Ghanimat was present at the hearing, his injuries clearly visible. The High Court ordered the Department for Investigation of Police Misconduct to investigate the case, but the Department subsequently concluded that "... the methods used on the petitioner complied with the approved interrogation procedures and had received the approval of the duly authorized officials". It recommended that no action be taken against the interrogators.

When 'Omar Ghanimat was released in July 1997, he had lost 17 kilograms in weight. He was unable to sit on a chair and he had no sensation in his forearms. In November 1997 he underwent surgery to treat his left knee, damaged by being forced to kneel in *gambaz*. In one doctor's opinion, he suffers from 10 per cent permanent disability as a result of torture.

Register to take action against torture at www.stoptorture.org

for instance, has defied numerous judgments by the Palestinian High Court requiring the release of individual prisoners. Hundreds of political detainees are held in Palestinian prisons without charge or trial on suspicion of collaborating with the Israeli authorities, or for suspected membership of Islamist groups opposed to the peace process with Israel. Many, if not most, of these detainees have been tortured or ill-treated. Prolonged incommunicado detention in the period after arrest has facilitated this abuse. For example, in August 1999, Sami Nawfel, a leading member of *Hizb al-Khalas*, a legal Islamist political party which has stated its opposition to violence, was arrested by members of General Intelligence. He was detained for eight days before being released without charge. He alleges that while he was detained he was beaten on the soles of his feet, painfully handcuffed, forced to hold contorted positions for long periods, and deprived of sleep. When Sami Nawfel was released, bruises, swellings and abrasions were visible on different parts of his body, particularly his limbs. A medical report confirmed injuries consistent with his allegations.

Torture is legalized: In 1987 the global campaign to eradicate torture suffered a setback when the Israeli government officially endorsed a Commission of Inquiry report which justified the use of "moderate physical pressure" during interrogation. Methods such as violent shaking and prolonged shackling in contorted positions had been used routinely by the security services against Palestinian detainees; both the practice and the harm caused were well known. The decision prompted intense debate within Israel about the use of torture and led to a national and international campaign to overturn the decision. Human rights activists argued that the use of torture could never be justified, either legally or morally, and that its effectiveness in preventing violent attacks by armed political groups had never been proved. In September 1999 the Israeli High Court ruled that such methods were unlawful and should be banned. A private member's bill to allow the General Security Service to use "physical pressure" during interrogation was brought before parliament later that year, but partly because of the strength of the national and international movement against the legalization of torture in Israel, this draft law has so far failed to gain enough support.

Impunity is enshrined in law: The most blatant form of legalized impunity is found in laws granting immunity from prosecution to those involved in acts of torture. These are often enacted during states of emergency or other situations where governments claim there is a special threat to law and order.

Many laws granting immunity from prosecution for torturers have been introduced in periods of political transition, for example following a period of military rule or as part of negotiations ending an armed conflict. Under these laws people known to have committed torture have been shielded from prosecution, ostensibly to promote national reconciliation. The argument that such measures are needed in order to guarantee the stability of the transition and in order for society's wounds to heal may seem a powerful one. But experience has shown that where justice is denied in the name of national reconciliation, a heavy price is paid by society as a whole, as well as by the victims and their relatives. In order to build a new social and legal order founded on strong human rights principles and the rule of law, the needs of justice and reconciliation must be recognized as complementary rather than mutually exclusive.

Amnesty laws or similar measures are contrary to international law if they are adopted before the truth of the crimes has been established, before the victims have been provided with reparation and before the judicial process has been completed with a clear verdict of guilt or acquittal. They lay a dangerous foundation for the future.

In Sierra Leone a blanket amnesty was provided for by the 1999 Lomé peace agreement which sought to end the bitter conflict. This amnesty allowed the perpetrators of gross human rights abuses, including the widespread and systematic use of torture, to evade justice. By failing to provide a deterrent to continuing human rights abuses by all sides, the agreement laid the foundation for renewed violence and abuses against the civilian population in 2000.

In South Africa a Truth and Reconciliation Commission (TRC) was established as a result of negotiations which ended *apartheid*. The TRC was given the power to grant amnesties where perpetrators of "politically motivated" human rights abuses, including torture, acknowledged their crimes and disclosed full details. Although the amnesties were justified by the authorities as necessary for securing a peaceful transition, many survivors and relatives have felt aggrieved at the latitude granted to the perpetrators. This sentiment has been exacerbated by the slowness with which the government has acted on the TRC's recommendations for reparations for the victims of human rights crimes. In its October 1998 report the TRC, however, vehemently opposed a proposed blanket amnesty "in order to avoid a culture of impunity and to entrench the rule of law".

> The Vienna Declaration adopted at the 1993 UN World Conference on Human Rights calls on all governments to "abrogate legislation leading to impunity for those responsible for grave violations of human rights such as torture and prosecute such violations, thereby providing a firm basis for the rule of law."

No other mechanisms to ensure accountability are available: Prosecution, although key, is only one of the steps that need to be taken to overcome impunity. Administrative and disciplinary sanctions are also important to drive home the message that torture is not an acceptable method of obtaining information or countering the threats that members of the security forces face in their work. Administrative regulations should allow for a prompt, thorough, independent and impartial hearing into all allegations of torture; the suspension of the officer involved from active duty pending investigation and their removal, transfer or dismissal if found responsible; together with other appropriate penalties, such as fines or the obligation to pay reparations.

How an institution responds internally to allegations that its personnel have used torture is crucial in undermining or reinforcing impunity. Promoting or rewarding an officer under investigation for torture clearly sends the message that such conduct is tolerated, even encouraged. Arguments that torture is an isolated occurrence by rogue officers – "rotten apples" – may prevent the institutionalized nature of the problem from being acknowledged or addressed. Some police authorities claim that criminal sanctions against police officers accused of torture will affect morale and further undermine their capacity to protect citizens against crime. Such a response fails to challenge the prevailing ethos within an institution which views torture as acceptable professional behaviour.

Civil litigation in many countries provides victims of torture with the possibility of suing for damages. Often civil suits are the only remedy left when criminal prosecution has been blocked. A civil suit can bring several benefits: important information may be disclosed in the course of the proceedings or damages may be awarded which not only benefit the victim materially, but can also amount to a tacit admission of responsibility. However, sometimes compensation is awarded as a means of ending judicial proceedings which are likely to lead to a judgment unfavourable to the state. Awarding compensation does not relieve the state of its obligation to ensure that criminal responsibility for the act of torture is established.

In some countries the authorities have been prepared to grant compensation to victims of torture, but have failed to bring the perpetrators to justice. Each year, the Supreme Court in Sri Lanka has awarded compensation to people who were tortured by the police. The largest known sum of compensation to date was awarded to Bathatha Jayatunga Gamage Malsha Kumari, a 14-year-old girl, who was tortured by police in Hambantota district in 1995. She was hung by her wrists from a tree and beaten with rubber hoses and sticks, apparently in order to make her confess to having stolen a piece of jewellery from a neighbour. The police went to extraordinary lengths to try and persuade her family to withdraw the compensation claim. They allegedly offered to pay the family a large sum of money and to file a case against the neighbour who made the complaint of theft. They also tried to get Bathatha to sign a document without allowing her mother to read it. They obtained a statement from her father stating he had not requested the lawyer to file a case in the Supreme Court. At a later stage, police even filed a case against the girl on a charge of threatening her neighbours. The Supreme Court, however, pursued the case, ultimately resulting in record compensation being awarded to her. The Supreme Court has repeatedly expressed its frustration at the lack of follow-up by relevant authorities to its recommendations for further investigations and appropriate action "by way of criminal proceedings or disciplinary action" against those involved in torture. So far, not a single perpetrator has been found guilty of torture in a court of law in Sri Lanka.

No safe haven for torturers

Torture is an international crime that requires an international response. Under the UN Convention against Torture, any state can and should judge anyone on its territory who is suspected of torture, regardless of the place where the crimes were committed, the nationality of the suspected perpetrator or the nationality of the victim.

The principle of *universal jurisdiction* requires states to bring suspected torturers in their territory to justice in their own courts or else to extradite them to a state able and willing to do so. This principle was established more than 50 years ago following the Second World War and was incorporated into the four Geneva Conventions of 1949. For decades it remained a dead letter, apart from trials for crimes committed during the Second World War, such as the Adolf Eichmann trial in Israel and the Imre Finta trial in Canada. Most states failed to give their courts such jurisdiction under national law. Those that did hardly ever exercised it. Political considerations always prevailed over those of principle. As a result perpetrators evading justice in their own countries have had little difficulty in finding "safe havens" elsewhere.

Recent developments, however, indicate that in future fewer countries will tolerate torturers on their soil. As a direct consequence of the establishment of the Yugoslavia Tribunal in 1993 and Rwanda Tribunal in 1994, states were spurred into action. Prosecutions on the basis of universal jurisdiction for recent crimes have taken place in Austria, Belgium, Denmark, France, Germany, the Netherlands, Spain and Switzerland. Germany and Italy have opened criminal proceedings into torture, extrajudicial executions and "disappearances" in Argentina in the 1970s and 1980s.

The case of Augusto Pinochet, the former Chilean military ruler who was arrested in the UK in October 1998, is the most well known of these cases. His arrest followed a request for his extradition to Spain to face charges of torture and other crimes. The arrest itself sent a powerful signal that no one suspected of such crimes can be above international law, even when national laws protect them from prosecution. Painstaking work by victims, their relatives, and lawyers had led to judicial investigations being initiated in Spain and to a request for extradition by the Spanish government. In accepting the extradition request, the UK courts confirmed the basic principle that people accused of torture can and should be prosecuted no matter where they happen to be. The UK House of Lords also firmly established that former heads of state are not immune from prosecution for such crimes:

"... torture is an international crime over which international law and the parties to the Torture Convention have given universal jurisdiction to all courts wherever the torture occurs."[26]

| Augusto Pinochet

The case also highlighted some of the hurdles involved in enforcing accountability internationally through universal jurisdiction. The restrictive scope of UK law meant that Pinochet could only be extradited to face charges of torture committed after 1988, the date when the UN Convention against Torture came into force in the UK. The fact that diplomatic and economic relations between the two countries were at stake heightened the risk of political interference in the judicial process to determine whether extradition should go ahead. The decision that Pinochet should be allowed to return to Chile on health grounds was taken by the Home Secretary, not by a court of law. Nevertheless, Augusto Pinochet's return to Chile has not meant that the struggle against impunity is lost. Instead the focus has shifted back to Chile, where the authorities must now remove the legal obstacles — including a 1978 amnesty law — to bringing torturers to justice. A promising first step was taken in August 2000, when the Chilean Supreme Court decided to lift the parliamentary immunity that Augusto Pinochet enjoyed as senator for life.

The momentum generated by the Pinochet case has rekindled hopes that the longstanding principle of universal jurisdiction for torture will increasingly become a reality in the 21st century. In July 1999, judicial authorities in France opened proceedings against Ely Ould Dha, an officer in the Mauritanian army arrested while attending a military course in Montpellier, France. The authorities intervened after human rights organizations presented a formal complaint to the police on behalf of two Mauritanian citizens who claimed they had been tortured by the officer in 1990 and 1991. The use of torture was widespread during that period as part of a pattern of mass expulsion of members of black communities. The French authorities declared that they had jurisdiction over the case under French legislation incorporating the provisions of the UN Convention against Torture. Unfortunately, he fled to Mauritania before a court could determine his guilt or innocence.

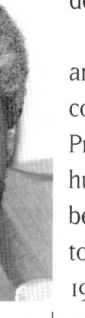

On 26 January 2000, a coalition of Chadian, African and international human rights groups filed a criminal complaint in Dakar, Senegal, against the former President of Chad, Hissein Habré, for crimes against humanity and torture committed during his rule between 1982 and 1990. Hissein Habré had been allowed to take up residence in Senegal after he was deposed in 1990, despite evidence that he had personally given orders to torture and kill. For nearly a decade, AI had repeatedly voiced its concern that the Senegalese authorities had made no moves to abide by their obligations under the UN Convention against Torture and ensure that Hissein Habré was brought to justice. On 28 January 2000, a Senegalese judge ruled that a judicial investigation into Hissein Habré's complicity in acts of torture should proceed. However, in July 2000, a Senegalese court ruled that it had no jurisdiction to prosecute Hissein Habré for crimes committed in Chad. The coalition of NGOs lodged an appeal against this decision.

Hissein Habré

AI is campaigning to make universal jurisdiction a meaningful tool in the fight against torture and other grave human rights violations. It has drawn up 14 principles to guide governments on the steps they need to take to ensure that universal jurisdiction can be effectively exercised by their national courts.[27]

International tribunals

Another major development in the search for more effective international mechanisms against impunity was the establishment by the UN of two international tribunals to prosecute those responsible for genocide, crimes against humanity and war crimes — including the systematic or widespread use of torture —

committed in the early 1990s in Rwanda and the former Yugoslavia. The functioning of these tribunals has been hampered by shortages of human and financial resources and lack of sufficient cooperation from individual states, for example in providing intelligence and assisting in the arrest of indicted suspects. However, despite such problems the tribunals have indicted and convicted a number of people on torture-related charges. They have ruled that when rape is committed as part of a widespread or systematic pattern of crimes against humanity it, too, is a crime against humanity. They have also ruled that rape constitutes an instrument of genocide if committed with the specific intent of destroying, in whole or in part, a national, racial, ethnic or religious group. Aiding and abetting outrages upon personal dignity, including rape, has been found by the International Criminal Tribunal for the former Yugoslavia to constitute a war crime.

An important step towards ending impunity was taken on 17 July 1998 when the international community agreed to establish a permanent international criminal court with jurisdiction over perpetrators of torture when it constitutes genocide, crimes against humanity or war crimes. The Rome Statute of the International Criminal Court enshrines the international community's stated resolve "to put an end to impunity for the perpetrators of these crimes" and recalled "that it is the duty of every State to exercise its criminal jurisdiction over those responsible for international crimes".

The International Criminal Court will not be a substitute for national courts able and willing to fulfil their responsibilities. It will exercise jurisdiction only when states fail to bring those responsible for these crimes to justice. The very existence of the Court should act as a catalyst to inspire national legal systems to fulfil their obligations, as well as being a deterrent for such crimes.

National legislatures in states which have signed and ratified the Rome Statute will need to enact legislation permitting the surrender of individuals indicted by the Court and requiring their authorities to cooperate with the Court.[28] When enacting such legislation, they should ensure that national courts can be an effective complement to the International Criminal Court. This must involve not only defining the crimes that fall within the Court's jurisdiction as crimes under national law in a manner consistent with definitions in the Rome Statute, but also providing their courts with universal

In July 1997, Bosnian Serb Dusan Tadić was sentenced to 20 years' imprisonment for war crimes and crimes against humanity, which included torture and cruel, inhuman or degrading treatment. He went on trial at the International Criminal Tribunal for the former Yugoslavia in the Hague, Netherlands.

jurisdiction over grave crimes under international law, including genocide, crimes against humanity, war crimes, extrajudicial executions, enforced "disappearances" and torture.

Such steps reinforce an integrated system of investigation and prosecution of crimes under international law and so will help reduce and, eventually, eliminate safe havens for those responsible for the worst crimes in the world.

The adoption of the Rome Statute and implementation by states of universal jurisdiction are landmarks in the struggle against impunity. They suggest that we are moving at last into a new era of enforcement of international law. These successes would not have been possible without the steadfast lobbying and painstaking groundwork done by victims, their relatives, lawyers and human rights activists. While the battle against impunity will continue to be fought primarily on the domestic front, these achievements point to the need for an increasingly globalized response to the challenge of pursuing torturers, wherever they may be.

العفـو الدوليـة

خروج
ممنوع دخول الشعارا
العفـو الدوليـة
AMNESTY INTERN

4: FIGHTING TORTURE: AN AGENDA FOR ACTION

"Amnesty International is making a big fuss about you. We won't do anything to you." This unusual assurance by Turkish security officers was given to five political detainees days after AI mobilized people around the world to send "urgent action" appeals to the Turkish authorities not to harm them. Unlike many other prisoners in Turkey held in similar circumstances, the five, who were arrested in March 2000, were not tortured in police and gendarmerie custody.

It is rare for those who take action against torture to know that their efforts have had an immediate effect. Change usually happens slowly and in piecemeal fashion, often as a result of the actions of diverse groups and constituencies. AI's work is usually only one small part of a much wider effort. However, in some countries there has been a decline in torture and ill-treatment, at least temporarily, after AI generated publicity and appeals. In others, the authorities have implemented AI recommendations such as improving official investigations into allegations of torture or incorporating human rights education into police training programs.

In some countries the work of AI and other human rights bodies has resulted in changes in the law, such as defining torture as a crime, and in judicial and administrative reforms. For example, criticisms by international organizations from outside Portugal were taken into account when the Portuguese Interior Ministry's General Inspectorate was set up in 1996/97 and when the Portuguese authorities devised new regulations on conditions of detention in police establishments. In a number of countries National Human Rights Commissions and Ombudspersons have been established in response to pressure from non-governmental organizations (NGOs). These institutions are often able to act on individual cases of torture and to address wider issues.

AI's work can help stimulate local action. For example, after AI published its report *Torture in Russia – This man-made Hell* in 1997,[29] local NGOs formed a coalition against torture and later that year the Russian

Lebanese AI members and former detainees of the Khiam detention centre, in south Lebanon, stretch torture free zone tape across the prison entrance. All detainees at this torture centre were liberated following the Israeli withdrawal from the occupied zone in May 2000.

President rescinded a decree which allowed incommunicado detention for up to a month. In Kenya AI has worked with a number of local NGOs which focus on torture. Ongoing work with doctors resulted in the creation of a standing committee on human rights within the Kenya Medical Association, which focuses on torture. AI has raised awareness of the extent of torture and ill-treatment with donor governments who have applied pressure on the Kenyan government to make improvements and have funded local NGOs working to combat torture. As a result of national and international campaigning, the Kenyan government ratified the UN Convention against Torture in 1997.

A father crouches with his two children beside a soldier in Kashmir, India. In the continuing conflict in the state of Jammu and Kashmir, Indian security forces have committed torture, "disappearances" and killings with impunity.

Much of the work of anti-torture activists focuses on helping individuals. Sometimes this entails trying to protect people taken into custody from torture. Sometimes it means action to stop torture once it has begun. Sometimes it involves helping torture survivors to gain redress by providing rehabilitation, or by giving assistance in legal cases to bring the perpetrators to justice.

In Bolivia, an AI delegation visited two prisoners held in isolation-punishment cells in the Chonchocoro high security prison in La Paz in June 2000. They had both been badly beaten by guards in an area near the prison governor's office, and feared that they would be killed — two other prisoners had been killed the evening before. AI issued an urgent action on behalf of the terrified men, and within hours appeals from around the world were reaching the authorities. Brazilian embassy staff paid a visit (one of the men is a Brazilian national) and a press conference was held to draw attention to torture and ill-treatment within the prison. At the end of July 2000, the two were still held in isolation, but the authorities were well aware of their responsibility for the prisoners' safety and of the international scrutiny of the case.

In Burundi, where torture is routinely inflicted on detainees, Jean Minani was charged with involvement in the murder of an army officer. The only evidence against him was his confession and the statement of a witness, both of which were extracted under torture. AI supported him by submitting photographs and other evidence of torture to the court where the case came to trial three years later. In court, the witness retracted her statement saying that it was false and she had only made it because she was afraid. Jean Minani was eventually acquitted because all the evidence against him was ruled inadmissible. He is now seeking compensation for illegal detention and torture.

NGO action against torture has strengthened enormously in recent decades. Many local and national human rights organizations have come into existence, denouncing the practice of torture and working to protect the victims. Complementing their efforts, new international NGOs have been formed, tackling torture from different perspectives. Six international NGOs have formed the Coalition of International NGOs against Torture (CINAT)[30], working together for the universal ratification of the UN Convention against Torture and raising awareness by organizing activities around the UN's International Day in Support of Victims of Torture on 26 June each year.

A new militancy and sense of common purpose among NGOs opposing torture emerged following an international conference in Stockholm in 1996, convened by AI. The conference marked a new phase in the fight against torture, a recognition that since governments had not done their job of stopping torture, it was time for NGOs to take a lead. One of the recommendations of the conference was that national NGOs in every country should draw up comprehensive plans for the abolition of torture, including legal and institutional reform, and training for those

Austria

Marcus Omofuma, a Nigerian national being forcibly deported from Austria, died after becoming unconscious on board a plane on 1 May 1999.

While the cause of his death remains in dispute, there is serious concern that the methods of restraint and level of force used by police officers on Marcus Omofuma when he resisted his deportation contributed to his death.

According to witnesses, Marcus Omofuma was bound and gagged like "a slaughtered animal" and carried on board the aircraft by police officers. Three officers then forced him into an empty row of seats at the back of the aircraft and strapped him down using adhesive tape; they wrapped "the entire upper part of his body and arms with adhesive tape, like a mummy". When he continued to protest, officers applied more adhesive tape to his chin and used a plastic belt to tie him further into the seat. One witness reported that "he was thrashing around wildly and trying over and over to get air. But the officials did nothing... The man appeared to be really fighting for his life."

MARCUS OMOFUMA

The flight was destined for Sofia, Bulgaria, from where the Austrian authorities had reserved a seat for Marcus Omofuma on a connecting flight to Lagos, Nigeria, on 2 May 1999. However, when the aircraft landed in Bulgaria, Marcus Omofuma was already unconscious. By the time a doctor arrived to treat him, he was dead. An autopsy, conducted in Bulgaria shortly after his death, concluded that Marcus Omofuma had died of asphyxia.

VIGIL HELD IN VIENNA IN MAY 2000, THE FIRST ANNIVERSARY OF MARCUS OMOFUMA'S DEATH.

More than one year later, the judicial investigation into Marcus Omofuma's death is still under way. It is still not clear to what extent the three police officers who accompanied Marcus Omofuma on the aircraft will be held responsible for their actions because of a dispute about the cause of death – a second autopsy, which was conducted in Austria, suggested that a previously undetected heart defect may have contributed to Marcus Omofuma's death.

Inquiries to date have revealed a considerable degree of ambiguity among police officers about the types of physical restraints which they believe they were permitted to use during deportations in May 1999. The Head of Vienna's Alien Police Branch reportedly banned the use of gagging in September 1998, stating that "deportees are to be returned to the police jail, if expulsion is only possible through the gagging of the mouth".

However, in May 1999, one of the three police officers accused of involvement in the deportation of Marcus Omofuma reportedly stated that everyone in his police department knew about the practice of gagging detainees during forcible deportations.

The Minister of the Interior issued a statement in May 1999 explicitly prohibiting the use of mouth gags. Amnesty International continues to press for clearer guidelines on the use of force and the types of restraints which may be employed during forcible expulsions.

Register to take action against torture at www.stoptorture.org

involved in the administration of justice. The conference also called for the adoption of comprehensive national legislation to prohibit and prevent torture, incorporating safeguards against torture in detention and access to remedies for victims and their dependants.

Preventing torture: safeguards in custody

AI has identified key safeguards in areas of law enforcement, the administration of justice and the prison system which can help to protect people against torture in custody. In country after country, AI has seen how the absence of these safeguards facilitates torture or ill-treatment. Even where they exist in law, they may be flouted. Preventing torture means not only ensuring that laws and procedural regulations incorporate safeguards, but also that they are respected in practice.

Torture often takes place during the first few hours or days of detention, and is facilitated if the detainee is held incommunicado – unable to contact people outside who could help them. In countries experiencing conflict or political unrest, the security forces sometimes have

The struggle for truth and justice can last for decades. Human rights activists in the 1990s continue to commemorate the victims of the "dirty war" in Argentina in the 1970s and early 1980s. The families of the many people who were detained, tortured and "disappeared" during the military governments continue to call for all those responsible to be brought to justice.

China

Abdulhelil Abdumijit was detained on 5 February 1997 in Gulja city, Xinjiang Uighur Autonomous Region (XUAR). He was beaten by police officers and taken to the local jail, where he was severely tortured to make him confess to his "crimes" and denounce his friends. He was made to face a wall and raise his arms while police officers beat his back. An official confirmed that Abdulhelil Abdumijit had been detained on suspicion of leading a demonstration, but the authorities have disclosed no further information about him. He was last reported to be detained in a prison run by the Xinjiang Construction and Production Corps 4th Division (the Bingtuan) outside Gulja, where he continued to be ill-treated; a prisoner witnessed a prison guard setting a dog on him.

Abdulhelil Abdumijit, a street trader, was one of hundreds of people who came out onto the streets of Gulja on 5 February 1997. The demonstrators waved banners and shouted slogans calling for an end to discrimination

ABDULHELIL ABDUMIJIT

against ethnic Uighurs. According to reports, after several hours of peaceful protest, armed police units arrived and arrested as many as 500 people. The following day a curfew was imposed on Gulja, riot squads were drafted in and the city was sealed off from the outside world for two weeks. Sporadic protests and rioting continued for several days. Scores of people were killed or injured in clashes between police and protesters, and thousands of protesters were believed to have been detained.

Particularly disturbing allegations have been made about the brutal treatment of people held in Gulja after the February 1997 protests and about the use in the XUAR of some forms of torture which, to Amnesty International's knowledge, are not being used elsewhere in China. There is a striking absence of official reports about prosecutions for torture in the XUAR – in sharp contrast with other parts of China. This suggests that the authorities are either ignoring or covering up widespread torture in the region, or may even have sanctioned its use in the context of repression.

Until 1949 the Uighurs, many of whom are Muslims, were the majority ethnic group in the XUAR; now they account for less than half of the population. Economic development in recent years has largely bypassed the Uighur population, who complain of discrimination in education and health care and suffer from high unemployment levels. At the same time, government policies have steadily eroded the Uighurs' social, economic and cultural rights. Since the late 1980s the government has also placed restrictions on their religious activities. Many mosques and religious schools have been closed down, and Muslims working in government offices are forbidden to practise their religion.

The forms of torture most frequently reported in the XUAR include severe beating and kicking; the use of electric batons; the use of handcuffs, shackles or ropes to tie prisoners in positions which cause intense pain; and exposure to extreme cold or heat. Other methods of torture reported in the XUAR, but not in the rest of the country, include the use of unidentified injections which cause the victim to become mentally unbalanced or to lose the ability to speak coherently; the insertion of pepper or chilli powder in the mouth, nose or genital organs; and the insertion of horse hair or wires into the penis.

Register to take action against torture at www.stoptorture.org

broad powers of arrest, often under emergency legislation, which may authorize long-term incommunicado detention. AI believes that the practice of incommunicado detention should be ended. Lawyers, relatives and doctors should be given access to prisoners without delay and regularly thereafter.

From the moment when they are deprived of their liberty, all prisoners should be immediately informed of their rights, including the right to lodge complaints about their treatment.

Judicial officials have a crucial role to play in preventing torture by exercising independent supervision over the process of detention. Anyone deprived of their liberty should be brought before a judge or other independent judicial authority without delay. The judge can see if there are any noticeable signs of ill-treatment, can hear any allegations by the prisoner and can order prompt, independent and confidential medical examination.

Another essential safeguard is the right to a judicial remedy, such as *habeas corpus* or *amparo*, which allow a court to protect a

Visits of inspection

There should be regular, independent, unannounced and unrestricted visits of inspection by appropriate bodies to all places of detention. The work of independent national bodies empowered to inspect places of detention has undoubtedly protected many people at risk of torture or ill-treatment. There is also an important role for visits by international bodies, such as the International Committee of the Red Cross, or regional bodies, such as the European Committee for the Prevention of Torture and Inhuman or Degrading Treatment or Punishment (CPT), established under the European Convention for the Prevention of Torture and Inhuman or Degrading Treatment or Punishment. Under the Convention, the CPT is empowered to make both periodic and unannounced visits, without restrictions, to any place of detention in any state party to the Convention (all 41 current member states of the Council of Europe). After a visit, the CPT transmits its findings to the state for comment, and these may be published if the state agrees. Since 1989, the CPT has made more than 100 country visits and the publication of CPT reports and states' responses has become a standard practice. At the UN, work is under way on an Optional Protocol to the UN Convention against Torture which would establish a similar system of visits of inspection on a global scale.

prisoner by having the prisoner brought before it or by visiting the place of detention.

The effectiveness of judicial supervision of detention depends on the extent to which arrest and detention can occur without judicial warrant; how courts respond to remedies such as *habeas corpus* or *amparo*; how the courts react in the face of evidence that a detainee has been tortured in custody; whether judges accept as evidence confessions or statements extracted under torture; and the powers of the judiciary to supervise and challenge the activities of the security services.

Other institutions — such as the Prosecutor's Office, National Human Rights Commissions, Ombudspersons or Ministerial Inspectorates — may also have a role in inspecting places of detention, determining the continuation of police custody or receiving complaints.

There must be no secret detention. Secret detention not only heightens the risk of torture, it can lead to "disappearance".

Torture or ill-treatment often occurs in the context of interrogation. In order to ensure a degree of independent supervision over the interrogating agency, the authorities responsible for detention should be separate from those in charge of interrogation. International standards require that a record be kept of the length of any interrogation, as well as the identity of the officials involved. Lawyers should be present during interrogations.

Women in custody should be held separately from men, and women should be attended and supervised only by women officers. Female detainees should have access to female doctors.

Children should be detained only as a last resort, and for the shortest time possible. When children are held in custody, they are entitled to special protective safeguards, founded on the duty of the state to secure the best interests of each child. For example, they should be held segregated from adults, except in cases where this would not be in the best interests of the child.

All complaints and all credible reports of torture must be officially investigated; those responsible must be brought to justice; the victims must be entitled to reparation, including compensation and rehabilitation.

These safeguards are set out in AI's 12-Point Program for the

Prevention of Torture by Agents of the State (see Appendix 1). The 12-Point Program is a tool to promote existing international standards and advance new standards, and a yardstick against which to measure the behaviour of governments.

Strategy-building

The struggle against torture has to be waged on many levels — local, national and international. While international interventions may support and reinforce domestic initiatives, they cannot replace them. When governments fail to live up to their commitment to abolish torture, human rights activists and others must take a lead.

AI strives to protect individual victims from torture and to press for longer-term change as an integral part of its everyday work. During this international campaign against torture, AI's members and supporters will redouble their own efforts and build new alliances to strengthen the fight. AI members in countries in every region of the world, with support from AI's International Secretariat, will join local NGOs to develop national strategies to combat torture. The aim is to forge links with human rights groups and with other organizations willing to become involved such as religious groups, trade unions, women's groups and professional associations. All these organizations have complementary capacities and expertise. Together with AI, they are well placed to identify the specific torture-related problems in their country or locality, to assess where pressure might most effectively be applied to achieve positive change, and so to develop a collective strategy for action.

No single strategy will be applicable to every situation. National strategies can encompass elements as various as campaigning for legal and institutional reform, lobbying the government to ratify UN and regional human rights treaties, raising awareness among the general public, human rights education, and action by partner organizations on individual cases (AI groups may not generally take action on individual cases in their own country).

In Peru, a collective of 61 human rights groups, the *Coordinadora Nacional de Derechos Humanos*, National

Coordinator for Human Rights, launched a nationwide campaign against torture in mid-1999. Political violence in Peru had declined substantially in the preceding period, but torture and police brutality against both criminal and political prisoners was widespread. The *Coordinadora* brought together organizations with different constituencies and agendas, such as women's groups focusing on domestic violence and other human rights groups (including AI Peru). They initiated a public education campaign around the slogan "No one has the right to ill-treat anyone — not your husband, not your teacher, not the police". During the campaign, local human rights and other groups are using a combination of dialogue and pressure to obtain commitments from police and mayors to end the torture and ill-treatment of prisoners. Police chiefs and mayors all over Peru are being urged to declare their district a "District Free of Torture and Ill-treatment".

The working relationships forged in the anti-torture struggle will endure beyond AI's intensive worldwide campaign against torture, and the strategies devised to combat torture in individual countries will underpin AI's work for years to come.

An interrogation room at the Tuol Sleng Museum in Phnom Penh, Cambodia. The building was formerly a security prison where members of the Communist Party were detained in appalling conditions by the Khmer Rouge from 1976 to the start of 1979.

Using the international system against torture

A range of international remedies may be used by victims of torture, particularly those who have been denied the possibility of justice in their own country. The UN has created an impressive body of mechanisms to monitor the steps taken by governments to combat torture and, in some cases, to consider individual complaints. Two regional courts, the Inter-American Court of Human Rights and the European Court of Human Rights, have adopted legally binding judgments on individual cases of torture and other violations of the regional human rights treaties under which they were created. Proceedings before these courts have served to stimulate action at the national level.

UN mechanisms for action against torture

UN mechanisms[31] aimed at stopping and preventing torture include the UN Committee against Torture, created under the UN Convention against Torture. It examines reports that states parties to the Convention are required to submit on their implementation of the Convention. It can also consider complaints by one state against another and complaints by individuals, provided that the state concerned has accepted these procedures. In addition, the Committee can act upon receiving reliable information that torture is being practised systematically, and this inquiry can include a visit to the state concerned.

Another important mechanism is the UN Special Rapporteur on torture, mandated by the UN Commission on Human Rights to report on the occurrence of torture and issues relevant to it. The Special Rapporteur's activities include sending urgent appeals in cases of imminent risk of torture, carrying out fact-finding missions, and reporting annually to the UN Commission on Human Rights.

Other UN bodies which can take action against torture include the Human Rights Committee, which examines reports presented by states parties to the International Covenant on Civil and Political Rights and considers individual complaints from countries which have ratified the first Optional Protocol to the Covenant; the Committee on the Rights of the Child, which reviews reports from states parties to the Convention on the Rights of the Child; other thematic mechanisms such as the Special Rapporteur on violence against women; and country-specific mechanisms of the UN Commission on Human Rights.

Abdurressak Ipek, a Kurd from south-east Turkey, has heard nothing of his two sons since they were arrested by the Turkish army in May 1994. The authorities have denied any knowledge of his sons' whereabouts but Ipek has regularly visited his local office of the Turkish Human Rights Association, hoping for news. The agony suffered by the relatives of the "disappeared" of not knowing what has happened to loved ones is in itself a form of torture or ill-treatment.

One example of the use of international mechanisms to combat torture, and of efforts to circumvent them, is the case of Ahmed Selmouni. Ahmed Selmouni, of dual Dutch and Moroccan nationality, was arrested in November 1991 by five police officers in Bobigny (Seine-Saint-Denis), France. While in their custody he was repeatedly punched and kicked, beaten with a truncheon and baseball bat, and forced to do physical exercise. He also claimed he had been sexually abused. Although Ahmed Selmouni had been arrested in 1991, the five officers involved were not examined by a judge until 1997. In March 1999 proceedings against France began before the European Court of Human Rights in Strasbourg. However, in February 1999, just six weeks before the opening of the case in Strasbourg, the officers appeared before a Versailles court, thereby allowing the French government to claim that domestic remedies had not been exhausted and that if the European Court were to deliver a judgment on the torture of Ahmed Selmouni, it would infringe the presumption of innocence. The European Court of Human Rights rejected the French government's arguments and in July 2000 found that France had violated Article 3 of the European Convention on Human Rights, which prohibits torture and inhuman or degrading treatment or punishment. The Court found that Ahmed Selmouni had clearly

New developments in anti-torture standards

Three important new human rights instruments are currently under consideration by the UN Commission on Human Rights. Each would contribute significantly to the fight against torture.

- The Optional Protocol to the UN Convention against Torture. This would provide for a global system of visits of inspection to places of detention. Any state ratifying the Optional Protocol would commit itself to allow international inspection visits to police stations, prisons and any other place in its territory where people are deprived of their liberty.
- The Basic Principles and Guidelines on the Right to a Remedy and Reparation for Victims of Violations of International Human Rights and Humanitarian Law. The rights of victims of human rights violations include the right of access to justice, the right to know the truth about the violations, and the right to reparation, the forms of which are spelled out in detail in the text.
- The Set of Principles for the Protection and Promotion of Human Rights through Action to Combat Impunity. Among other measures needed to overcome impunity, this sets out elements of the right of victims to justice and provides guidelines for extrajudicial commissions of inquiry into human rights violations, including "truth commissions" set up after periods of intense political repression come to an end.

Progress on the three proposed instruments has been slow in the face of opposition by some states. Crucial elements of the Optional Protocol in particular are still in dispute. The Commission on Human Rights should move quickly to adopt the three standards in the strongest possible form.

"endured repeated and sustained assaults over a number of days of questioning". It stated that the physical and mental violence inflicted "caused 'severe' pain and suffering and was particularly serious and cruel".

In the Versailles court, the five officers denied the charges of committing violence and sexual assault against Ahmed Selmouni and another man, Abdemajid Madi, and suggested that the two men had injured themselves or had perhaps watched too many films. However, the Versailles court convicted all five officers and sentenced them to between two and four years' imprisonment. All immediately appealed. An unusually swift appeal drastically cut the "exemplary" four-year prison term imposed on one of the officers to 18 months, of which 15 were suspended. The convictions against the four other officers were cut to suspended prison sentences of between 10 and 15 months. The prosecutor attached to the appeal court had herself controversially requested that the officers be "returned their honour" and declared not guilty of the offence of sexual assault and that, if they were to remain convicted of violent acts, they should benefit from an amnesty. The court upheld the convictions against the officers for violent acts but set aside the conviction for sexual assault.

The battle for hearts and minds

Public opinion can be an effective control mechanism against torture and a curb on impunity, even in repressive countries. If there is widespread outrage when a case of torture is exposed, officials are more likely to order an investigation and act on its findings. If, on the other hand, the response appears to be one of indifference, those practising torture will feel free to continue. Human rights activists have a critically important role in making the public aware when torture is inflicted, and in insisting that it can never be justified.

Today, it is becoming increasingly clear that tacit support for torture is a problem, particularly when the victim is a member of a despised group — perhaps a homeless teenager, a drug addict or a thief. Few people will say "I support torture", but many accept or even welcome the use of "tough methods" against certain types of people at certain times. The challenge is to establish that those who face discrimination, the marginalized and the criminal have human rights, just like everybody else. It has to be made clear that torture is unacceptable in all circumstances.

As part of the preparations for this campaign against torture, AI collaborated with the international opinion polling company Gallup International to assess public attitudes. In August and September 1999, Gallup International interviewed over 50,000 people in 60 countries. This Millennium Survey is the largest survey ever made of world opinion.

One question asked whether the right not to be tortured was respected in their own country: 31 per cent of respondents said it

Torture worldwide — the knowledge gap

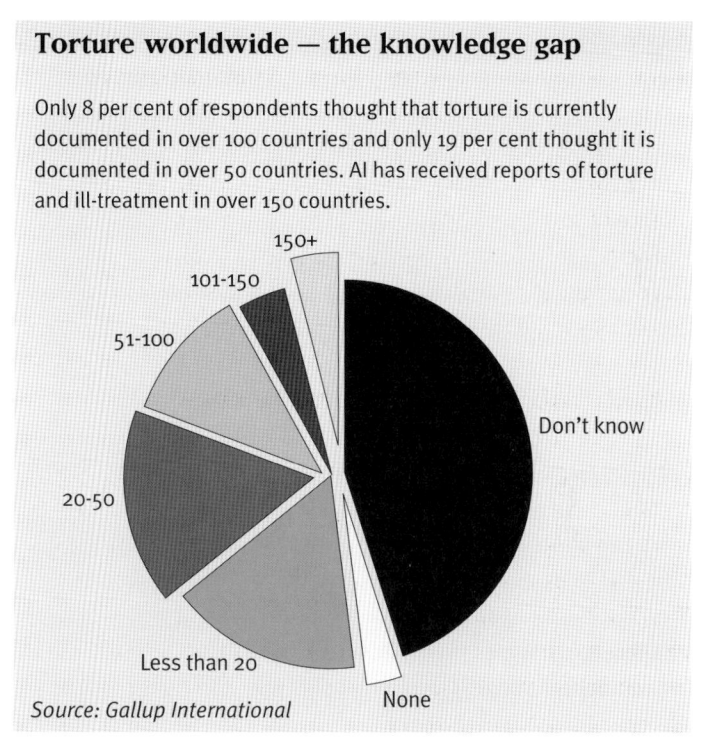

Only 8 per cent of respondents thought that torture is currently documented in over 100 countries and only 19 per cent thought it is documented in over 50 countries. AI has received reports of torture and ill-treatment in over 150 countries.

Segments: 150+, 101-150, 51-100, 20-50, Less than 20, None, Don't know

Source: Gallup International

was fully respected, 37 per cent said only partially respected and 21 per cent said "not respected".

When asked what measures would be "very effective" or "quite effective" in reducing or eliminating torture, 77 per cent of respondents cited more prosecutions; 75 per cent cited greater public awareness; 70 per cent cited stricter control of the police; 70 per cent cited stricter international laws; and 65 per cent cited grassroots campaigning. This last figure represents a potential audience of hundreds of millions of people who believe that campaigning against torture can be effective, and whom we seek to reach and to mobilize into action.

The task of winning public opinion to oppose torture in all its guises involves a series of challenges including obtaining information, involving local NGOs, and reaching out to people who influence policy and public opinion. A human rights education program can develop public awareness and appreciation of human rights. Knowledge of human rights, and the laws and practices which delimit them, can build community resistance to abuses. Human rights education should be an element integrated into the broader education curriculum — and should form part of the training of police, prison guards, soldiers, journalists, lawyers and medical professionals. Public attitudes may be influenced by the portrayal of official violence in the news and entertainment media.

Public opinion is never static, and the arguments against torture have to change with changing perceptions and changing times. Today, those engaged in opposing torture have to stand up for the rights of "unpopular" groups. We have to show the pernicious effects of ill-treatment so routine it goes virtually unnoticed. We have to take a principled stand against torture and ill-treatment whenever and wherever it occurs.

Stopping the torture trade

"The torturers had just left but the horror remained. There was the whipping pole and the window grilles where prisoners were tied naked for days, freezing water thrown over them at night. Then there were the electric leads for the little dynamo – the machine mercifully taken off to Israel by the interrogators – which had the inmates shrieking with pain when the electrodes touched their fingers or penises. And there were the handcuffs which an ex-prisoner handed to me yesterday afternoon.

"Engraved into the steel were the words: 'The Peerless Handcuff Co. Springfield, Mass. Made in USA.' And I wondered, in Israel's most shameful prison, if the executives over in Springfield knew what they were doing when they sold these manacles.

"They were used over years to bind the arms of prisoners before interrogation. And they wore them, day and night, as they were kicked..."[32]
Journalist Robert Fisk describing Khiam detention centre after the Israeli withdrawal from south Lebanon in May 2000.

The governments and companies who train and arm torturers around the world cause untold human misery. Around the world manufacturers and salesmen have profited from the trade in torture and all too often they have been able to rely on the complicity of governments.

Most of the world's military and security exports come from a select group of countries which includes Bulgaria, China, France, Germany, Israel, Romania, the Russian Federation, South Africa, Ukraine, the UK and the USA. This list includes the five permanent members of the UN Security Council.

Some of the tools of the torturer's trade seem almost medieval – shackles, leg irons, thumbscrews, handcuffs and whips. However, in recent years there has been a marked expansion in the use of electro-shock technology.

Torturers around the world often prefer using electric shock torture because they believe it will not leave permanent marks as evidence on their victims' bodies, and so makes their crimes less easily detectable.

Roberto (not his real name) was arrested by the state security forces in Zaire (now the Democratic Republic of the Congo) in 1991. His captors started by beating him with sticks. But an officer stopped them, saying "it will leave scars and we will get complaints from Amnesty International". He ordered his men to use an electro-shock baton instead.

"This time they worked on me again with the electric baton on the nape of the neck and in the genitals and it hurt so much that even now when I speak it is difficult to keep my head still as the back of my neck hurts so much... This type of weapon... those people who make it for torture, they don't test it on their own bodies and they don't know the pain it causes. They do it to make other people suffer quite simply to make money."

Nearly a decade later, despite international treaties and conventions banning torture, high pulse and high voltage electro-shock weapons are still in use around the world. Since 1990 electro-shock torture and ill-treatment have been reported in at least 58 countries including Angola, Algeria, India, Indonesia, Mexico, the Philippines, Russia, Saudi Arabia, Sri Lanka, Turkey, the USA and Yugoslavia. In more than 20 countries, hand-held

Khiam detention centre, south Lebanon. De Gaulle Boutros stands by an electricity pylon from which he was suspended with a hood over his head, doused with water, given electric shocks and beaten with electric cables.
In May 2000 the gates of Khiam detention centre were forced open and the last 144 prisoners released. Detainees at the centre run by the South Lebanon Army militia in cooperation with the Israeli army were routinely tortured.

electro-shock batons specifically designed for use on human beings have been used.

Electro-shock stun technology was initially developed in the USA during the 1970s and this country still continues to lead the way in the trade. AI research has uncovered 78 US companies that have manufactured, marketed, bought or sold electro-shock devices. This technology comes in many shapes and forms, such as electro-shock shields, batons, stun guns... even "tasers", which fire fishhook darts connected to wires and allow users to shock people from a distance.

One of the most sinister developments has been the stun belt. A stun belt is worn by its victim, sometimes for hours on end. A 50,000 volt shock, lasting eight seconds, can be set off by flicking a switch up to 300 feet away. The shock causes incapacitation in the first few seconds, and severe pain which intensifies during the eight seconds. Wendell Harrison, given shocks during his trial in the USA in 1996, described an "excruciating pain as if a long needle had been inserted up

> "This is the worst thing – an electric cattle prod. They use this on your body. If they press that button, your whole body will be in shock... They used it all the time on my body. They tortured me because I was speaking out for independence and I will continue to speak out." Palden Gyatso, a Tibetan monk who had spent 33 years in Chinese prisons and labour camps, displays the type of instruments of torture used on him.

through [my] spine and into the base of [my] skull". Two years later he was still suffering from nightmares and sleep loss as a result. Stun belts are widely used as instruments of restraint on prisoners in the USA. AI believes that the mental anguish caused by wearing the belt and the constant fear of its activation is in itself cruel, inhuman and degrading. AI has therefore specifically called for the belt to be banned immediately. In May 2000 the UN Committee against Torture recommended that the US "abolish electro-shock stun belts".

The immediate effects of electric shock torture vary, but include severe pain, loss of muscle control, nausea, convulsions, fainting and involuntary defecation and urination. Muscle stiffness and long term damage to teeth and hair have also been documented, as well as devastating mental scars sometimes leading to severe depression and impotence.

The human rights records of previous recipients of such devices only serve to heighten AI's concerns. An investigation of US Commerce Department documents published in *Time Magazine* in April 1998 found that "a dozen shipments of stun guns and shock batons" had been approved "over the past decade to Saudi Arabia", a country where electro-shock torture has been recorded.

Electro-shock technology may have begun in the USA, but it is now a global industry. AI's research shows that during the last decade more than 120 companies, operating in 22 countries, have manufactured, sold, advertised or sought to procure electro-shock weapons.

In 1995 the managing director of a Scottish company, ICL Technical Plastics, admitted selling electro-shock batons to China in 1990, stating that: "The Chinese wanted to copy them." Chinese factories now mass produce electro-shock batons and reports indicate that Chinese companies have exported electro-shock weapons to Cambodia and Indonesia — both countries where electro-shock torture has been documented by AI. One of those on the receiving end of electro-shock torture was Indonesian political activist, Pius Lustrilanang. In February 1998, he spoke of his ordeal: "I had electric shocks applied to my feet and hands for so long they had to change the batteries, and I became so weak I told them what they wanted."

Despite the inherent dangers in the spread of these weapons, which can so easily be turned into instruments of torture, there appears to be little or no effective regulation by governments of this trade. AI is campaigning for the immediate global suspension of the manufacture, export and use of electro-shock weapons until independent medical investigations have been carried out into their effects and operation.

The global trade in military and security equipment requires stringent national and international controls. These controls must be clear, detailed and comprehensive in order to ensure that states cannot export equipment, training or personnel to customers who might use them to violate human rights.

In Kenya the police have used tear gas, batons, plastic bullets and water-cannon to drive peaceful pro-democracy activists from the streets. For example, in July 1997 Kenyan paramilitary police stormed the All Saints Anglican Cathedral in Nairobi. First they threw tear gas canisters, then they moved in wielding truncheons. Several dozen peaceful pro-reform advocates sheltering inside were left bleeding and badly hurt; many more were injured. AI obtained some of the tear gas canisters and plastic bullets used against peaceful protesters in Kenya in 1997. The canisters and plastic bullets were traced back to manufacturers in the UK.

AI members swung into action, putting pressure on the UK government and the companies concerned to stop their trade in equipment used in repression. Subsequently the UK government declared that it had rejected £1.5 million of licence applications for riot control equipment – including batons and tear gas – to Kenyan police because of human rights concerns.

In June 1999, 2,000 peaceful demonstrators calling for democratic change in Kenya were charged by police on horseback. Police then beat demonstrators with sticks and fired tear gas into the crowd. The police later moved in with water-cannon which fired a mixture of water and tear gas directly into crowds who had nowhere to run. The manufacturer of the tear gas this time was a French-based company. The Kenyan authorities had been able to find alternative sources for equipment which they could use to violate human rights.

Protecting people fleeing from torture

Torture is a global phenomenon and there are few countries where torture survivors have not sought refuge. It has been estimated that 20 to 30 per cent of the world's 15 million refugees are torture victims.[33]

In theory, refugees who have fled their country in fear of torture are entitled to international protection. They should be granted asylum, so protecting them from being returned to their torturers. However, in practice this often does not happen.

Muthuthamby Vanitha, a young woman from Sri Lanka, sought asylum in France. Her application was rejected, and she was deported back to Sri Lanka in October 1998. She was detained by Sri Lankan police upon her arrival, released and then arrested again after a short period. Her mother visited her in Kotahena police station, Colombo, and Muthuthamby Vanitha said she had been hit with iron pipes and had swollen legs because she had been refused access to the toilet. She said that after a visit from a lawyer, police slapped her in the face and hit her all over her body. She was warned that if she complained again, she would be hung upside down and tortured systematically.

According to international refugee law, Muthuthamby Vanitha should have been protected from being sent back to Sri Lanka. No one should face forcible return (*refoulement*) to a country where they would be at risk of serious human rights violations, under the terms of the 1951 UN Convention relating to the Status of Refugees (the Refugee Convention) and its 1967 Protocol. The Refugee Convention protects people who have a "well-founded fear of persecution", including by non-state actors, and torture and ill-treatment fall squarely within the boundaries of what is considered to be persecution.

Other international human rights treaties also protect people from being sent back to danger. The UN Convention against Torture specifically prohibits the expulsion, return or extradition of anyone to a state "where there are substantial grounds for believing that he would be in danger of being subjected to torture". Unlike the Refugee Convention, which excludes certain people from protection as a refugee based on their past activities (such as serious crimes), under the UN Convention against Torture no one,

Iran

Akbar Mohammadi was arrested in Tehran in July 1999 during clashes between students and the security forces. He was initially held in incommunicado detention in Towhid under the jurisdiction of the Ministry of Intelligence before being transferred to Evin prison in March 2000.

While in detention he was reportedly handcuffed, suspended by his arms, and whipped on the soles of his feet with electric cables. Prison guards reportedly beat him until he was on the point of losing consciousness, saying that all he had to do was to blink to accept the charges against him.

After being sentenced to death in a secret trial, Akbar Mohammadi wrote to the head of the judiciary, Mahmud Hashemi-Shahrudi, stating that while in detention he had been "violently beaten"; the letter was published in a number of Iranian newspapers.

AKBAR MOHAMMADI

© Student Movement Coordination Committee for Democracy in Iran

According to reports, Akbar Mohammadi went on a hunger strike in protest at his detention and was said to be suffering from possible kidney failure. He was reportedly not allowed to receive hospital treatment despite referral to hospital by the prison doctor.

Akbar Mohammadi was one of hundreds of people arrested following violent clashes in Tehran in July 1999. The events leading up to the clashes began on 8 July with a peaceful demonstration by students who gathered outside their university dormitories to protest against the closure of the daily newspaper *Salam*. They were attacked by armed members of *Ansar-e-Hezbollah*, a militant group; members of the security forces at the scene took no action to protect the students.

Some hours later, members of the security forces and *Ansar-e-Hezbollah* forced their way into the student dormitories. At least one person died and hundreds were reportedly wounded. In the days that followed there was a dramatic increase in the scale of the demonstrations, the level of violence rose, and unrest spread to a number of provincial cities.

Brigadier General Farhad Nazari, commander of the security forces at the time, and 19 police officers were charged in connection with the storming of the student dormitories on 8 July 1999. In proceedings against them, which began in February 2000, several students gave evidence alleging that they had been brutally attacked by members of the police and by vigilante groups.

Akbar Mohammadi may have been targeted for arrest because of the connection with his brother, Manuchehr Mohammadi, who was accused of orchestrating the unrest and was later forced to "confess" to involvement with "counter-revolutionary agents" on Iranian state television.

Akbar Mohammadi was reportedly sentenced to death in September 1999 after a secret trial by a Revolutionary Court in Tehran whose procedures do not conform to international standards of fair trial. His sentence was reportedly upheld by the Supreme Court, but was subsequently commuted to 15 years' imprisonment by order of the Leader of the Islamic Republic of Iran.

Register to take action against torture at www.stoptorture.org

regardless of who they are, may be returned to a country where they are at risk of torture.

When someone manages to escape their country and applies for asylum, the decision on whether to grant refugee status is taken by the individual receiving state. But governments' willingness to offer asylum has fallen sharply in recent years. Many governments are devoting their energies to keeping refugees away from their borders, or are treating them harshly in the hope that others will be deterred from seeking asylum. Some states that have traditionally hosted large numbers of refugees are turning them away because of the international community's failure to share the responsibility and cost of refugee protection. Many states are applying an increasingly restrictive interpretation of the Refugee Convention. The result is that people fleeing torture are being returned to their persecutors.

Some rejected asylum-seekers have appealed to the UN Committee against Torture, the committee of experts which monitors states' compliance with the UN Convention against Torture. For example, Pauline Muzonzo Paku Kisoki, an opposition party member from Zaire (now Democratic Republic of the Congo), sought asylum in Sweden. She said she had escaped from a Zairean prison where she had been held for more than a year, raped more than 10 times, regularly beaten with whips made from tyres and with batons, and burned with cigarettes. The Swedish authorities rejected her claim on the grounds that there were contradictions and inconsistencies in her story, and argued that conditions in Zaire had improved enough to send her back. The UN Committee against Torture concluded in 1996 that she would still be at risk of torture if returned, and that Sweden should not return her. The Committee noted that "complete accuracy is seldom to be expected by victims of torture".[34] After vigorous campaigning by NGOs, the Swedish authorities allowed her to stay in Sweden.

For a small number of individuals, the UN Committee against Torture can provide protection if their asylum application has been rejected – but this can never be a substitute for fair and satisfactory national asylum procedures. Between November 1990 and September 1999, the Committee had expressed views on 34 cases,[35] but there are more than a million people seeking asylum around the world. The Committee can only hear petitions from people in states which have made a declaration under Article 22 of the Convention allowing individual communications. As of July 2000, only 41 states had done so.

Refugees fleeing human rights violations often face further dangers as they try to escape. A group of around 1,100 members of the ethnic Karen minority in Myanmar escaped to Thailand in 1997 after the Burmese security forces destroyed their homes and forcibly relocated members of their community. The Thai authorities ordered them to return to Myanmar and Thai soldiers dragged people from their shelters, kicking and beating them with rifle butts. In the panic, a three-day-old baby was dropped and died from a broken neck.

Even when refugees reach a "safe" country, they are not necessarily safe. States are retreating from their obligations to protect refugees and are increasingly violating asylum-seekers' human rights in an effort to press them to abandon their asylum claims and to deter other would-be asylum-seekers. In many countries asylum-seekers are detained indefinitely on grounds beyond those allowed by international standards, which state that detention should normally be avoided. Often they are held in conditions that amount to ill-treatment. Asylum-seekers are held in insanitary and overcrowded cells. They are shackled, confined with criminal prisoners, and exposed to physical and sexual assault. Hunger-strikes to protest against dire conditions, and suicides, are on the increase.

The prevalence of torture worldwide means that men, women and children continue to seek asylum in order to escape it. The effort to ensure that they receive protection is an integral part of the fight against torture.

Medical professionals and torture

The participation of doctors in systematic, mass torture during the Second World War was deeply shocking to the public at large and to the medical community itself. Determination never to allow such atrocities to be repeated was a major thrust behind the development of the Universal Declaration of Human Rights and also provided the initial impetus for the evolution of international

Gathering medical evidence: the Istanbul Protocol

Accurate, detailed information is indispensable in the fight against torture. The absence of solid documentation to support and substantiate allegations by torture victims allows governments to deny the truth and evade their responsibilities. The Manual on Effective Investigation and Documentation of Torture and Other Cruel, Inhuman or Degrading Treatment or Punishment, known as the Istanbul Protocol,[36] provides guidelines on how to assess and document medical evidence of torture. Drafted by forensic scientists, doctors, human rights monitors and lawyers from 15 countries, the Istanbul Protocol was adopted in 1999.

The Istanbul Protocol provides detailed medical and legal guidelines on the assessment of individual allegations of torture and ill-treatment, as well as on reporting the findings of such investigations to the judiciary and other bodies. The documentation methods contained in the manual include a range of medical, psychological and laboratory procedures. The Istanbul Protocol also outlines minimum standards which states should meet when they investigate complaints of torture. The "Principles on the Effective Documentation of Torture and Other Cruel, Inhuman or Degrading Treatment or Punishment" have been adopted and published by the UN[37] and provide a framework for medical investigation of torture allegations. The Istanbul Protocol gives guidance to NGOs in their anti-torture work, and sets standards by which to assess official investigations.

codes of medical ethics. In 1949, the World Medical Association first adopted an International Code of Medical Ethics, setting out doctors' obligation to practise for the good of their patients and never to do harm. Since then, numerous bodies, including the World Medical Association, the International Council of Nurses and the World Psychiatric Association have elaborated codes of ethics prohibiting the involvement of medical personnel in torture. In 1982, the UN adopted the Principles of Medical Ethics relevant to the Role of Health Personnel, particularly Physicians, in the Protection of Prisoners and Detainees against Torture and Other Cruel, Inhuman or Degrading Treatment or Punishment.

Numerous national medical associations have taken a stand against torture. Both the Chilean and Turkish medical associations have played a role in investigating allegations that doctors were involved in torture. However, their recent history highlights some of the problems faced by health professionals. The Chilean Medical Association only regained the right to elect its own leaders in the early 1980s, after nearly 10 years of government-imposed officers. During the previous decade the Association had, according to its own records, "disclaimed reports that physicians were present during the torture or ill-treatment of detainees held in centers run by the security forces."[38] Since the 1980s, the Association has produced its own ethical code which contains clear and detailed instructions for doctors dealing with prisoners. In Turkey, six members of the executive committee of the Turkish Medical Association were subjected to a long trial on political charges after writing to the government in 1985 calling for doctors to be relieved of their role in executions. The code of ethics drafted the following year by the Turkish Medical Association prohibits involvement in torture and presence at an execution.[39] The Association has been forthright in its condemnation of medical participation in torture in Turkey, and has actively promoted international ethical standards.

Treatment of torture survivors

"...Not everyone they torture survives to tell the story of what she or he endured. Nevertheless, there are those who did survive. For many of us, survival is far worse than the actual torture. No part of our lives has been untouched. We readily recognize that not only are we victims of this crime, but our families, our communities and our societies are as well.

"Survivors meet each new day with fear, despair, mistrust and, amazingly, hope. It is this hope that empowers us to confront torture wherever it exists."
Torture Abolition and Survivors Support Coalition, May 2000

The widespread use of torture in the 1970s in South American countries where health workers' organizations were well developed and politically aware led to the establishment of local groups working to provide medical and psychological care to victims. Providing this kind of practical help often involved taking great personal risks, given the repressive conditions in which many were forced to operate. At the same time, thousands of traumatized refugees were arriving in North America and Europe. Health professionals from the exiled communities, working together with local practitioners, responded to the manifest needs of the refugees. The work of AI medical groups, the first of which started in Denmark in 1974, gave an additional impulse to these initiatives. Within a few years there were more than 4,000 doctors in 34 countries organized in AI's medical groups.

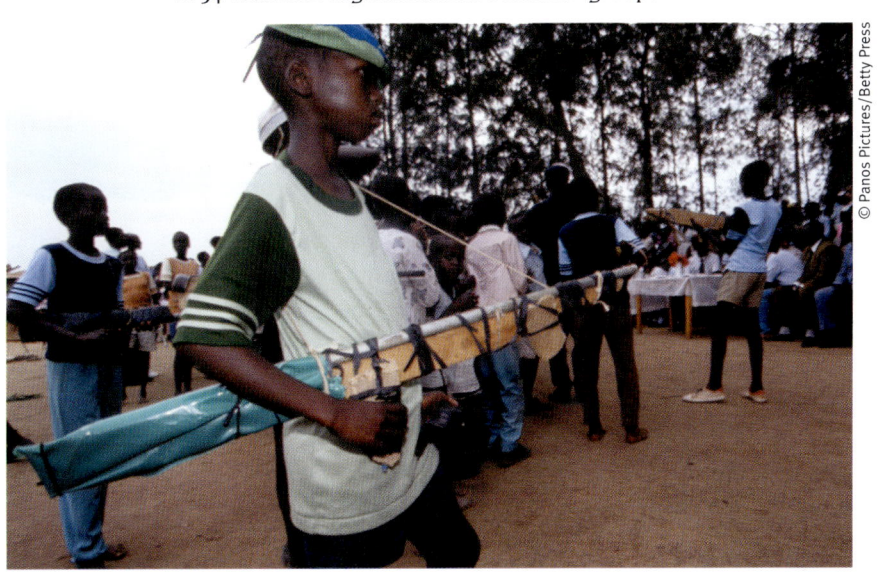

Children at this Unaccompanied Children's Centre in Rwanda undergo role-play therapy to help them overcome the trauma of conflict.

Over the past quarter of a century there has been a major expansion in this work and currently there are some 200 therapeutic groups working in all continents to provide specialist care to survivors of torture. They have conducted a great deal of research into the physical and psychological after-effects of torture.

"We have developed different rehabilitation models which are used at many centres and programs worldwide... A point of conceptual importance is that we are not considering torture survivors to be sick, but simply to have normal reactions to a very abnormal event."
Inge Kemp Genefke, Secretary General, International Rehabilitation Council for Torture Victims, 1999

The support these groups give to torture survivors goes beyond care and rehabilitation for their physical injuries. People skilled in many different disciplines are involved — nurses, doctors, physical therapists, psychologists, and many others. Treatment centres allow survivors of torture to express their grief and anger in an environment where they know they will be safe and their experiences will be believed.

An Iraqi man arrived at the Medical Foundation for the Victims of Torture in London, UK, complaining of pains in his head and back. He often wished he could kill himself — especially on Tuesdays. Tuesdays were unbearable for him. In the course of treatment he revealed that his son and brother had been executed on a Tuesday, and he had been forced to watch. When he asked to kiss his son's body, he was brutally beaten. Part of his route to recovery was to spend Tuesdays alone in a room thinking about his son, trying to remember what his son looked like and what they had shared. It was an important step in his struggle to recognize that his sense of guilt and helplessness were misplaced, that he could have done nothing to save him and that he could now lay the boy's memory to rest.[40] For both the carer and the victim, treatment is a journey — it has to be as creative as the ingenious cruelty of the torturer.

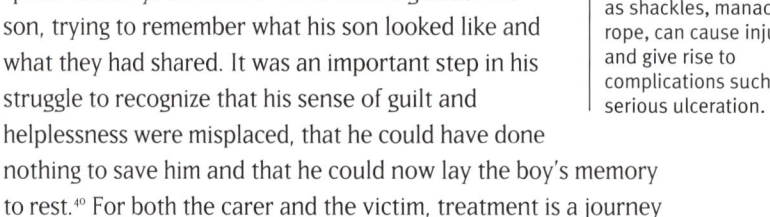

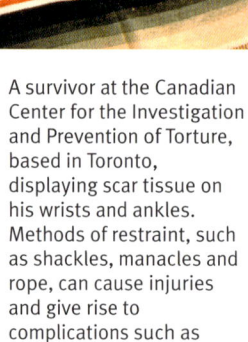

A survivor at the Canadian Center for the Investigation and Prevention of Torture, based in Toronto, displaying scar tissue on his wrists and ankles. Methods of restraint, such as shackles, manacles and rope, can cause injuries and give rise to complications such as serious ulceration.

"Inside I felt I had nothing to live for. I was on the point of giving up. After all I had been through, I was very depressed… It was staff at the Medical Foundation who persuaded me to fight on. They made me realize that if I didn't, my abusers would have won."
Survivor of torture, Kenya[41]

Recommendations

Ending torture is a collective responsibility. Most of the following recommendations are directed at governments as they have the obligation, as well as the means, to bring about change and ensure respect for human rights. But NGOs, members of various professions and ordinary people also have important roles to play.

How can torture be ended? It is not simply a matter of changing national laws: most forms of torture and ill-treatment are already illegal. Eradicating torture must be understood in the broader sense of doing away with an unlawful and unacceptable practice. This means working towards permanent vigilance on the part of the institutions of government and civil society. It means implementing reforms to ensure that torture cannot persist as a routine practice. It means that if isolated cases of torture should occur, there is a strong reaction from the public and the authorities which prevents the torturer from torturing again and which deters others from committing similar acts. Then we will be able to say that torture is virtually unthinkable and that we have come as close as humanly possible to eradicating torture from the face of the earth.

These recommendations reflect the focus of **Take a step to stamp out torture** — AI's latest campaign against torture. The campaign aims to achieve progress in three interrelated areas — preventing torture, confronting discrimination and overcoming impunity.

Preventing torture

Governments are obliged under international law to respect and to ensure the right to freedom from torture and ill-treatment under all circumstances.

1. The highest authorities should condemn torture in all its forms whenever it occurs. They must make clear to all members of the security forces and judiciary that torture will never be tolerated. The leaders of armed political groups must also make clear to their forces that torture is always unacceptable.

2. Torture should be expressly prohibited in law, in line with the UN Convention against Torture and other international standards. States should also ensure that their laws do not condone or allow impunity for acts by non-state actors that may amount to torture.
3. Torture should be condemned by opinion leaders, professional associations and members of the public, as a means of putting pressure on the authorities to stop it. The news and entertainment media should refrain from portraying torture in a way that seeks to justify it or makes it seem acceptable.
4. People deprived of their liberty are vulnerable to torture and ill-treatment. The measures needed to protect prisoners are well known, and AI has brought together the most important measures which governments should take in a 12-Point Program for the Prevention of Torture by Agents of the State (see Appendix 1). Governments must now implement these measures.
5. Female prisoners should be held separately from male prisoners and supervised by female members of staff. Female security personnel should be present during the interrogation of women detainees, and should be solely responsible for conducting body searches. Rape of women in custody by public officials should always be recognized as an act of torture.
6. The treatment of children who come into contact with the law must be in line with international standards on the administration of juvenile justice. Children in custody must be segregated from adults, except where this would not be in the best interests of the child.
7. The authorities should ensure that the policies and practices of law enforcement agencies on the treatment of detainees and the use of force conform to international standards including the UN Convention against Torture, the UN Code of Conduct for Law Enforcement Officials and the UN Basic Principles on the Use of Force and Firearms by Law Enforcement Officials.
8. Governments should ban methods of restraint which are known to cause severe suffering and endanger life such as choke-holds. Leg irons and electro-shock stun belts should be banned. The use of other electro-shock devices should be suspended pending the outcome of rigorous, independent and impartial investigations into their use and effects.

9. Amputation, flogging and all other corporal punishments imposed by the courts as penal sanctions should be abolished in law. The infliction of such punishments should cease immediately. All administrative corporal punishments, including corporal punishment in schools, should be abolished as well.
10. The authorities responsible for prisons and other places of detention must take urgent measures to improve conditions which are life-threatening or pose a serious risk to prisoners' health. These include severe overcrowding, lack of adequate food and drink, lack of adequate sanitary facilities, exposure to extremes of heat or cold, exposure to infectious disease and denial of medical care to ill prisoners. The authorities should ensure that conditions of detention conform to international standards, including the UN Standard Minimum Rules for theTreatment of Prisoners.
11. All countries should ratify, without reservations, the UN Convention against Torture with declarations under Articles 21 and 22 allowing for inter-state and individual complaints. All reservations to the Convention should be withdrawn. Countries should also ratify the other international and regional treaties which provide for the prevention and punishment of torture, including the International Covenant on Civil and Political Rights and its first Optional Protocol, which provides for individual complaints.
12. UN member states should press for speedy adoption of the strongest possible Optional Protocol to the UN Convention against Torture, providing for a global system of inspection visits to places of detention as a safeguard against torture. NGOs should press governments to work for its adoption.
13. The UN Committee against Torture should ensure that the questions it puts to state representatives on their country's performance in preventing torture and the recommendations it makes are as effective as possible and should monitor closely the implementation of its recommendations. NGOs and the news media should publicize these sessions of the Committee. Governments should implement the Committee's recommendations and those of the UN Special Rapporteur on torture.

14. Human rights defenders working to combat torture should be enabled to pursue their legitimate activities without fear of arrest or attack.
15. NGOs should encourage victims of torture and their families to submit individual cases to the UN Committee against Torture or the Human Rights Committee if the individual complaints procedures under the two relevant treaties are available in their countries, and to the relevant regional bodies. Urgent information on individuals facing torture should be sent to the UN Special Rapporteur on torture or the UN Special Rapporteur on violence against women for action.
16. Governments should make the worldwide eradication of torture a matter of their foreign policy. They should instruct their missions in other countries to monitor the incidence of torture, to intercede with the authorities in individual cases and to press for the necessary changes in legislation and practice.
17. Governments should ensure that transfers of equipment and training for military, security or police use do not facilitate torture.
18. Governments should ensure that no one is forcibly returned to another country where he or she risks being tortured, including where the state fails to protect against torture by non-state actors. The detention of asylum-seekers should normally be avoided. Where detention is lawful, the authorities should ensure that asylum-seekers are not subjected to cruel, inhuman or degrading treatment.

Combat discrimination

Tackling discrimination is an important means of preventing torture. Discrimination creates a climate permitting or encouraging torture or ill-treatment. It also undermines the principle of equal protection of the law to all, facilitating impunity for torture.

19. All countries should ratify international and regional treaties which seek to strengthen protection against the torture or ill-treatment of members of particular groups. These include the UN Convention on the Elimination of All Forms of Discrimination against Women and its Optional Protocol which

provides for individual complaints; the International Convention on the Elimination of All Forms of Racial Discrimination; the Convention on the Rights of the Child; and the International Convention on the Protection of the Rights of All Migrant Workers and Members of their Families.

20. Governments should bring their laws and policies into line with the treaties cited above and repeal laws which breach the fundamental principle of non-discrimination. Governments should also implement the recommendations for preventing torture made by the monitoring bodies set up under these treaties, as well as by other experts such as the Special Rapporteur on violence against women and the Special Rapporteur on contemporary forms of racism, racial discrimination, xenophobia and related intolerance.

21. The authorities should ensure that training programs for law enforcement personnel include training on the prevention of violence against women, on the rights of the child and on discrimination on such grounds as race and sexual orientation.

22. The authorities should establish effective independent mechanisms to monitor the actions of law enforcement officials so that complaints of torture, ill-treatment and discrimination within the criminal justice system can be properly investigated and appropriate remedies implemented. They should also establish systems for effective consultation and coordination with relevant NGOs, including community groups and victim support groups. Monitoring bodies should maintain and publish uniform and comprehensive statistics on complaints of torture, ill-treatment and discrimination by law enforcement personnel.

23. Governments should comply with their international obligations to prevent, investigate, prosecute, punish and provide redress for violence against women, including violence that constitutes torture. The commitments to eradicate violence against women made by governments at the UN World Conference on Women in Beijing, China in 1995, and reaffirmed at the Beijing +5 Conference in June 2000, should be implemented as a matter of urgency.

24. Governments should also act with due diligence to protect children, women, racial and sexual minorities and other

groups facing discrimination against violence at the hands of non-state actors. As a first step, all such forms of violence should be criminalized and penalties should be commensurate to the gravity of the crime. Obstacles to the effective investigation and prosecution of alleged perpetrators and to providing redress to victims should be removed.

Overcome impunity

Governments are obliged under international law to bring those responsible for torture to justice and to cooperate with others in this effort. Impunity for torturers encourages the continued practice of torture, denies victims their rights and undermines the rule of law.

25. Those responsible for torture must be brought to justice. Complaints and reports of torture must be promptly, impartially, independently and thoroughly investigated. When there is sufficient admissible evidence, the suspect should be prosecuted. Proceedings must conform to international standards for a fair trial. Those found guilty must be punished by sanctions commensurate with the seriousness of the offence, but excluding the death penalty, which is itself a human rights violation. Civil suits and disciplinary measures should be used in addition to prosecution.

26. Victims of torture have a right to reparation including rehabilitation, compensation, restitution, satisfaction and guarantees that the crime will not be repeated. Governments should ensure that specialized treatment programs are available in countries where there are torture survivors and that victims of torture have an enforceable right to fair and adequate compensation. The dependants of people who have died under torture must also be entitled to compensation.

27. Victims and their families must be given access to the mechanisms of justice in order to obtain redress for the harm which they have suffered. They must be informed of their rights in seeking redress. Special measures should be implemented to ensure that women who have been the victims of torture or ill-treatment, including rape and other sexual

A corporal from the Canadian army points at the body of a Somali teenager who was tortured and killed by Canadian soldiers. In 1994, seven Canadian soldiers were court-martialled in connection with the killing of Shidane Abukar Arone in 1993. One was convicted of manslaughter and sentenced to five years' imprisonment. In 1996 there were allegations that officers in the Canadian army were involved in a cover-up of abuse by soldiers of Somalis during the 1992-1993 UN peacekeeping mission. A Commission of Inquiry was set up to investigate the allegations and alleged abuses by the Canadian Airborne Regiment during its mission to Somalia. The Regiment was disbanded for its part in the torture and deaths of Somali citizens.

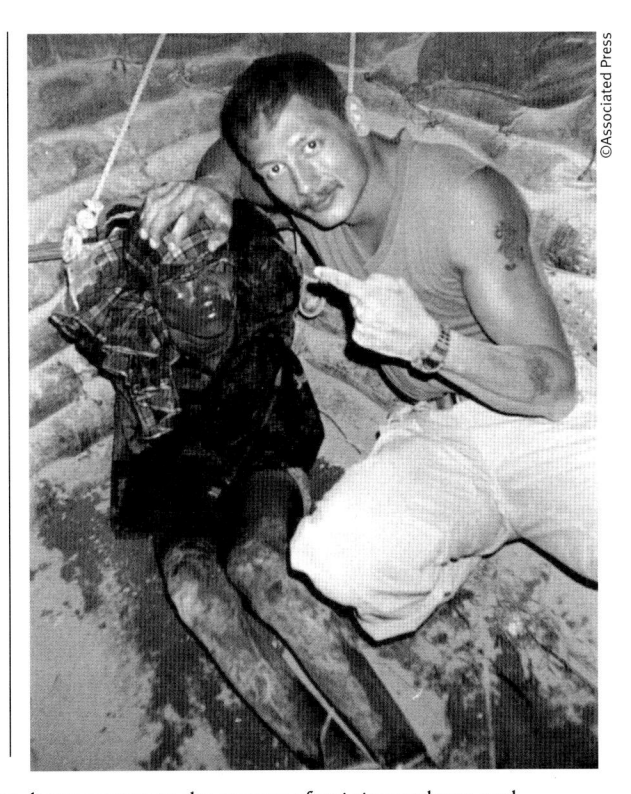

©Associated Press

abuse, have access to the means of gaining redress and obtaining reparation.

28. States should ensure that their legislation permits courts to exercise universal jurisdiction, so that suspected torturers in their territory can be brought to justice in their own courts, or extradited to a state able and willing to do so, in a fair trial without the possibility of the death penalty. Alleged torturers should be brought to justice wherever they may be, whatever their nationality or position, regardless of where the crime occurred and the nationality of the victim, and no matter how much time has elapsed since the crime was committed.

29. States should ratify the Rome Statute of the International Criminal Court and enact the necessary national legislation to implement it effectively.

WHAT YOU CAN DO

- Join our campaign – **Take a step to stamp out torture**
  You can help stamp out torture. Add your voice to Amnesty International's campaign. Help us to make a difference. Contact your national office of Amnesty International and ask for information about how to join the campaign, including information on how to take action on some of the specific cases featured in this report.
- Become a member of Amnesty International and other local and international human rights organizations which fight torture
- Make a donation to support Amnesty International's work
- Tell friends and family about the campaign and ask them to join too

Campaigning Online

The website **www.stoptorture.org** allows visitors to access AI's information about torture. It will also offer the opportunity to appeal on behalf of individuals at risk of being tortured. Those registering onto the site will receive urgent e-mail messages alerting them to take action during the campaign.

- Register to take action against torture at **www.stoptorture.org**

☐ I would like to join your campaign. Please send me more information.
☐ I would like to join Amnesty International. Please send me details.
☐ I would like to donate to Amnesty International's campaign to stamp out torture.

Credit card number: ☐☐☐☐ ☐☐☐☐ ☐☐☐☐ ☐☐☐☐

Expiry date _____ / _____   £_____ [amount]

Signature _____

Name _____

Address _____

_____

Please photocopy this coupon and send it to:
Amnesty International, International Secretariat, Campaign against Torture, 1 Easton Street, London WC1X 0DW, United Kingdom

Creating Torture Free Zones

Around the world, AI members and other human rights activists press their authorities to declare Torture Free Zones. One of the many ways of attracting attention is to wrap public buildings, former detention centres and other places of symbolic significance with Torture Free Zone tape.

Ukraine

Australia

Peru

Appendix 1. AI's 12-Point Program for the Prevention of Torture by Agents of the State

Amnesty International

12-Point Program for the Prevention of Torture by Agents of the State

Torture is a fundamental violation of human rights, condemned by the international community as an offence to human dignity and prohibited in all circumstances under international law.

Yet torture persists, daily and across the globe. Immediate steps are needed to confront torture and other cruel, inhuman or degrading treatment or punishment wherever they occur and to eradicate them totally.

Amnesty International calls on all governments to implement the following 12-Point Program for the Prevention of Torture by Agents of the State. It invites concerned individuals and organizations to ensure that they do so. Amnesty International believes that the implementation of these measures is a positive indication of a government's commitment to end torture and to work for its eradication worldwide.

1. Condemn torture
The highest authorities of every country should demonstrate their total opposition to torture. They should condemn torture unreservedly whenever it occurs. They should make clear to all members of the police, military and other security forces that torture will never be tolerated.

2. Ensure access to prisoners
Torture often takes place while prisoners are held incommunicado — unable to contact people outside who could help them or find out what is happening to them. The practice of incommunicado detention should be ended. Governments should ensure that all prisoners are brought before an independent judicial authority

without delay after being taken into custody. Prisoners should have access to relatives, lawyers and doctors without delay and regularly thereafter.

3. No secret detention

In some countries torture takes place in secret locations, often after the victims are made to "disappear". Governments should ensure that prisoners are held only in officially recognized places of detention and that accurate information about their arrest and whereabouts is made available immediately to relatives, lawyers and the courts. Effective judicial remedies should be available at all times to enable relatives and lawyers to find out immediately where a prisoner is held and under what authority and to ensure the prisoner's safety.

4. Provide safeguards during detention and interrogation

All prisoners should be immediately informed of their rights. These include the right to lodge complaints about their treatment and to have a judge rule without delay on the lawfulness of their detention. Judges should investigate any evidence of torture and order release if the detention is unlawful. A lawyer should be present during interrogations. Governments should ensure that conditions of detention conform to international standards for the treatment of prisoners and take into account the needs of members of particularly vulnerable groups. The authorities responsible for detention should be separate from those in charge of interrogation. There should be regular, independent, unannounced and unrestricted visits of inspection to all places of detention.

5. Prohibit torture in law

Governments should adopt laws for the prohibition and prevention of torture incorporating the main elements of the UN Convention against Torture and Other Cruel, Inhuman or Degrading Treatment or Punishment (Convention against Torture) and other relevant international standards. All judicial and administrative corporal punishments should be abolished. The prohibition of torture and the essential safeguards for its prevention must not be suspended under any circumstances, including states of war or other public emergency.

6. Investigate
All complaints and reports of torture should be promptly, impartially and effectively investigated by a body independent of the alleged perpetrators. The methods and findings of such investigations should be made public. Officials suspected of committing torture should be suspended from active duty during the investigation. Complainants, witnesses and others at risk should be protected from intimidation and reprisals.

7. Prosecute
Those responsible for torture must be brought to justice. This principle should apply wherever alleged torturers happen to be, whatever their nationality or position, regardless of where the crime was committed and the nationality of the victims, and no matter how much time has elapsed since the commission of the crime. Governments must exercise universal jurisdiction over alleged torturers or extradite them, and cooperate with each other in such criminal proceedings. Trials must be fair. An order from a superior officer must never be accepted as a justification for torture.

8. No use of statements extracted under torture
Governments should ensure that statements and other evidence obtained through torture may not be invoked in any proceedings, except against a person accused of torture.

9. Provide effective training
It should be made clear during the training of all officials involved in the custody, interrogation or medical care of prisoners that torture is a criminal act. Officials should be instructed that they have the right and duty to refuse to obey any order to torture.

10. Provide reparation
Victims of torture and their dependants should be entitled to obtain prompt reparation from the state including restitution, fair and adequate financial compensation and appropriate medical care and rehabilitation.

11. Ratify international treaties
All governments should ratify without reservations international treaties containing safeguards against torture, including the UN Convention against Torture with declarations providing for individual and inter-state complaints. Governments should comply with the recommendations of international bodies and experts on the prevention of torture.

12. Exercise international responsibility
Governments should use all available channels to intercede with the governments of countries where torture is reported. They should ensure that transfers of training and equipment for military, security or police use do not facilitate torture. Governments must not forcibly return a person to a country where he or she risks being tortured.

This 12-Point Program was adopted by Amnesty International in October 2000 as a program of measures to prevent the torture and ill-treatment of people who are in governmental custody or otherwise in the hands of agents of the state. Amnesty International holds governments to their international obligations to prevent and punish torture, whether committed by agents of the state or by other individuals. Amnesty International also opposes torture by armed political groups.

Appendix 2. International standards against torture (extracts)

Universal Declaration of Human Rights
"No one shall be subjected to torture or to cruel, inhuman or degrading treatment or punishment." (Article 5)

International Covenant on Civil and Political Rights
"No one shall be subjected to torture or to cruel, inhuman or degrading treatment or punishment. In particular, no one shall be subjected without his free consent to medical or scientific experimentation." (Article 7)

International Covenant on Civil and Political Rights
"All persons deprived of their liberty shall be treated with humanity and with respect for the inherent dignity of the human person." (Article 10)

European Convention for the Protection of Human Rights and Fundamental Freedoms
"No one shall be subjected to torture or to inhuman or degrading treatment or punishment." (Article 3)

American Convention on Human Rights
"No one shall be subjected to torture or to cruel, inhuman, or degrading punishment or treatment. All persons deprived of their liberty shall be treated with respect for the inherent dignity of the human person." (Article 5)

African Charter on Human and Peoples' Rights
"Every individual shall have the right to the respect of the dignity inherent in a human being and to the recognition of his legal status. All forms of exploitation and degradation of man, particularly slavery, slave trade, torture, cruel, inhuman or degrading punishment and treatment, shall be prohibited." (Article 5)

UN Declaration on the Protection of All Persons from Being Subjected to Torture and Other Cruel, Inhuman or Degrading Treatment or Punishment
"No State may permit or tolerate torture or other cruel, inhuman or degrading treatment or punishment." (Article 3)

UN Convention against Torture and Other Cruel, Inhuman or Degrading Treatment or Punishment
"Each State Party shall take effective legislative, administrative, judicial or other measures to prevent acts of torture in any territory under its jurisdiction." (Article 2)

Inter-American Convention to Prevent and Punish Torture
"The States Parties shall ensure that all acts of torture and attempts to commit torture are offenses under their criminal law and shall make such acts punishable by severe penalties that take into account their serious nature." (Article 6)

UN Body of Principles for the Protection of All Persons under Any Form of Detention or Imprisonment
"No person under any form of detention or imprisonment shall be subjected to torture or to cruel, inhuman or degrading treatment or punishment." (Principle 6)

UN Standard Minimum Rules for the Treatment of Prisoners
"Corporal punishment, punishment by placing in a dark cell, and all cruel, inhuman or degrading punishments shall be completely prohibited as punishments for disciplinary offences." (Rule 31)

Convention on the Rights of the Child
"No child shall be subjected to torture or other cruel, inhuman or degrading treatment or punishment..." (Article 37)

United Nations Rules for the Protection of Juveniles Deprived of their Liberty
"All disciplinary measures constituting cruel, inhuman or degrading treatment shall be strictly prohibited, including corporal punishment, placement in a dark cell, closed or solitary confinement or any other punishment that may compromise the physical or mental health of the juvenile concerned." (Article 67)

United Nations Rules for the Protection of Juveniles Deprived of their Liberty
"No member of the detention facility or institutional personnel may inflict, instigate or tolerate any act of torture or any form of harsh, cruel, inhuman or degrading treatment, punishment, correction or discipline under any pretext or circumstance whatsoever." (Article 87)

International Convention on the Elimination of All Forms of Racial Discrimination
"In compliance with the fundamental obligations laid down in article 2 of this Convention, States Parties undertake ... to guarantee the right of everyone, without distinction as to race, colour, or national or ethnic origin, to equality before the law, notably in the enjoyment of the following rights:

"(b) The right to security of person and protection by the State against violence or bodily harm, whether inflicted by government officials or by any individual group or institution..." (Article 5)

International Convention on the Protection of the Rights of All Migrant Workers and Members of Their Families
"No migrant worker or member of his or her family shall be subjected to torture or to cruel, inhuman or degrading treatment or punishment." (Article 10)

International Convention on the Protection of the Rights of All Migrant Workers and Members of Their Families
"Migrant workers and members of their families shall be entitled to

effective protection by the State against violence, physical injury, threats and intimidation, whether by public officials or by private individuals, groups or institutions." (Article 16.2)

UN Declaration on the Elimination of Violence against Women
"Women are entitled to the equal enjoyment and protection of all human rights and fundamental freedoms in the political, economic, social, cultural, civil or any other field. These rights include, *inter alia*:

"(h) The right not to be subjected to torture, or other cruel, inhuman or degrading treatment or punishment." (Article 3)

UN Code of Conduct for Law Enforcement Officials
"No law enforcement official may inflict, instigate or tolerate any act of torture or other cruel, inhuman or degrading treatment or punishment..." (Article 5)

UN Principles of Medical Ethics relevant to the Role of Health Personnel, particularly Physicians, in the Protection of Prisoners and Detainees against Torture and Other Cruel, Inhuman or Degrading Treatment or Punishment
"It is a gross contravention of medical ethics, as well as an offence under applicable international instruments, for health personnel, particularly physicians, to engage, actively or passively, in acts which constitute participation in, complicity in, incitement to or attempts to commit torture or other cruel, inhuman or degrading treatment or punishment." (Principle 2)

Geneva Conventions of August 12, 1949 (common Article 3)
"...the following acts are and shall remain prohibited at any time and in any place whatsoever with respect to the above-mentioned persons:
"(a) violence to life and person, in particular... mutilation, cruel treatment and torture;

"(c) outrages upon personal dignity, in particular humiliating and degrading treatment..."

Appendix 3. UN Convention against Torture, ratifications, declarations and reservations

States which have ratified or acceded or succeeded to the Convention are parties to the treaty and are bound to observe its provisions. States which have signed but not yet ratified have expressed their intention to become a party at some future date; meanwhile they are obliged to refrain from acts which would defeat the object and purpose of the treaty.

(At 30 June 2000)	Convention against Torture and Other Cruel, Inhuman or Degrading Treatment or Punishment	Declaration under Article 21 (Countries making a declaration under Article 21 recognize the competence of the UN Committee against Torture to consider inter-state complaints.)	Declaration under Article 22 (Countries making a declaration under Article 22 recognize the competence of the UN Committee against Torture to consider individual complaints.)
Afghanistan	x(28)		
Albania	x		
Algeria	x	x	x
Andorra			
Angola			
Antigua and Barbuda	x		
Argentina	x	x	x
Armenia	x		
Australia	x	x	x
Austria	x	x	x
Azerbaijan	x		
Bahamas			
Bahrain	x		
Bangladesh	x		
Barbados			
Belarus	x(28)		
Belgium	x	x	x
Belize	x		
Benin	x		
Bhutan			
Bolivia	x		
Bosnia and Herzegovina	x		
Botswana			

Brazil	x		
Brunei Darussalam			
Bulgaria	x(28)	x	x
Burkina Faso	x		
Burundi	x		
Cambodia	x		
Cameroon	x		
Canada	x	x	x
Cape Verde	x		
Central African Republic			
Chad	x		
Chile	x		
China	x(28)		
Colombia	x		
Comoros			
Congo (Democratic Republic of the)	x		
Congo (Republic of the)			
Costa Rica	x		
Côte d'Ivoire	x		
Croatia	x	x	x
Cuba	x		
Cyprus	x	x	x
Czech Republic	x	x	x
Denmark	x	x	x
Djibouti			
Dominica			
Dominican Republic	s		
Ecuador	x	x	x
Egypt	x		
El Salvador	x		
Equatorial Guinea			
Eritrea			
Estonia	x		
Ethiopia	x		
Fiji			
Finland	x	x	x
France	x	x	x
Gabon	s		
Gambia	s		
Georgia	x		
Germany	x		
Ghana			
Greece	x	x	x
Grenada			
Guatemala	x		
Guinea	x		
Guinea-Bissau			
Guyana	x		

Haiti			
Holy See			
Honduras	x		
Hungary	x	x	x
Iceland	x	x	x
India	s		
Indonesia	x		
Iran (Islamic Republic of)			
Iraq			
Ireland	s		
Israel	x(28)		
Italy	x	x	x
Jamaica			
Japan	x	x	
Jordan	x		
Kazakstan	x		
Kenya	x		
Kiribati			
Korea (Democratic People's Republic of)			
Korea (Republic of)	x		
Kuwait	x		
Kyrgyzstan	x		
Lao People's Democratic Republic			
Latvia	x		
Lebanon	x		
Lesotho			
Liberia			
Libyan Arab Jamahiriya	x		
Liechtenstein	x	x	x
Lithuania	x		
Luxembourg	x	x	x
Macedonia (former Yugoslav Republic of)	x		
Madagascar			
Malawi	x		
Malaysia			
Maldives			
Mali	x		
Malta	x	x	x
Marshall Islands			
Mauritania			
Mauritius	x		
Mexico	x		
Micronesia (Federated States of)			
Moldova	x		
Monaco	x	x	x
Mongolia			
Morocco	x(28)		
Mozambique	x		

Country				
Myanmar				
Namibia	x			
Nauru				
Nepal	x			
Netherlands	x	x	x	
New Zealand	x	x	x	
Nicaragua	s			
Niger	x			
Nigeria	s			
Norway	x	x	x	
Oman				
Pakistan				
Palau				
Panama	x			
Papua New Guinea				
Paraguay	x			
Peru	x			
Philippines	x			
Poland	x	x	x	
Portugal	x	x	x	
Qatar	x			
Romania	x			
Russian Federation	x	x	x	
Rwanda				
Saint Kitts and Nevis				
Saint Lucia				
Saint Vincent and the Grenadines				
Samoa				
San Marino				
Sao Tome and Principe				
Saudi Arabia	x			
Senegal	x	x	x	
Seychelles	x			
Sierra Leone	s			
Singapore				
Slovakia	x	x	x	
Slovenia	x	x	x	
Solomon Islands				
Somalia	x			
South Africa	x	x	-x	
Spain	x	x	x	
Sri Lanka	x			
Sudan	s			
Suriname				
Swaziland				
Sweden	x	x	x	
Switzerland	x	x	x	
Syrian Arab Republic				

Tajikistan	x		
Tanzania			
Thailand			
Togo	x	x	x
Tonga			
Trinidad and Tobago			
Tunisia	x	x	x
Turkey	x	x	x
Turkmenistan	x		
Tuvalu			
Uganda	x		
Ukraine	x(28)		
United Arab Emirates			
United Kingdom	x	x	
United States of America	x	x	
Uruguay	x	x	x
Uzbekistan	x		
Vanuatu			
Venezuela	x	x	x
Viet Nam			
Yemen	x		
Yugoslavia (Federal Republic of)	x	x	x
Zambia	x		
Zimbabwe			

s denotes that country has signed but not yet ratified

x denotes that country is a party, either through ratification, accession or succession. **x** is also used to indicate countries that have made declarations under articles 21 or 22 of the Convention.

(28) Countries making a reservation under Article 28 do not recognize the competence of the UN Committee against Torture to undertake confidential inquiries into allegations of systematic torture if warranted.

ENDNOTES

1 Article 5 of the Universal Declaration of Human Rights.

2 The nickname of a guard described by Adrien Wayi as "particularly ferocious".

3 *Singapore: Cruel Punishment* (AI Index: ASA 36/03/91). Caning is still carried out in Singapore for a range of criminal offences.

4 The definition of torture in Article 1 of the UN Convention against Torture specifically excludes pain and suffering arising from "lawful sanctions".

5 Human Rights Committee, General Comment 20, 1992, para. 5.

6 UN Commission on Human Rights Resolution 2000/43, adopted 20 April 2000 (annex).

7 Report of the UN Special Rapporteur on torture, UN Doc. E/CN.4/1997/7, para. 6.

8 *Pakistan: Honour killings of girls and women* (AI Index: ASA 33/18/99).

9 *Female Genital Mutilation: A Human Rights Information Pack* (AI Index: ACT 77/05/97)

10 *Israel: Human rights abuses of women trafficked from countries of the former Soviet Union into Israel's sex industry* (AI Index: MDE 15/17/00).

11 Human Rights Committee, General Comment 20, 1992.

12 Case of *A v. the United Kingdom* (application 25599/94).

13 The standard of due diligence was applied by the Inter-American Court of Human Rights in its judgment in 1988 on the Velásquez-Rodríguez case: "An illegal act which violates human rights and which is initially not directly imputable to the State (for example, because it is an act of a private person or because the person responsible has not been identified) can lead to international responsibility of the State, not because of the act itself but because of the lack of due diligence to prevent the violation or to respond to it as required by the Convention." This standard has been incorporated into international instruments and elaborated on by human rights experts and mechanisms of the UN as well as by national courts.

14 CCPR/C/79/Add.93 Concluding Observations/Comments, adopted on 28 July 1998, para. 16.

15 *Bosnia-Herzegovina — How can they sleep at night?* Arrest Now! (AI Index: EUR 63/22/97).

16 See, for example, the International Convention on the Elimination of All Forms of Racial Discrimination, the Convention on the Elimination of All Forms of Discrimination against Women, the Declaration on the Elimination of All Forms of Intolerance and of Discrimination Based on Religion or Belief and the Convention on the Rights of the Child.

17 The International Convention on the Elimination of All Forms of Racial Discrimination refers to discrimination based on "race, colour, descent, or national or ethnic origin".

18 The International Convention on the Protection of the Rights of All Migrant Workers and Members of Their Families was adopted by the UN in 1990, but by October 2000 had not yet come into force because not enough countries had ratified it.

19 The Declaration on the Elimination of Violence against Women defines such violence as "any act of gender-based violence that results in, or is likely to result in, physical, sexual, or psychological harm or suffering to women, including threats of such acts, coercion or arbitrary deprivation of liberty, whether occurring in public or private life". It includes "violence perpetrated or condoned by the State wherever it occurs" and "violence occurring in

the family" and the "general community".

20 See *Sierra Leone: Rape and other forms of sexual violence against girls and women* (AI Index: AFR 51/35/00).

21 Report to the Commission on Human Rights 26 January 1998 (E/CN.4/1998/54).

22 See for example the Declaration on the Elimination of Violence against Women; General Recommendation No. 19 and the Concluding Observations of the Committee on the Elimination of Discrimination against Women (CEDAW); the Inter-American Convention on the Prevention, Punishment and Eradication of Violence against Women ("Convention of Belém do Pará"). See also the recommendations of the UN Special Rapporteur on violence against women.

23 Asma Jahangir is the current UN Special Rapporteur on extrajudicial, summary or arbitrary executions.

24 *Public Scandals: Sexual Orientation and Criminal Law in Romania,* International Gay and Lesbian Human Rights Commission/Human Rights Watch, 1998.

25 Convention on the Rights of the Child, Article 37; UN Standard Minimum Rules for the Administration of Juvenile Justice ("Beijing Rules"); UN Guidelines for the Prevention of Juvenile Delinquency ("Riyadh Guidelines").

26 *Regina v. Bartle ex parte Pinochet,* House of Lords, 24 March 1999.

27 See *Universal Jurisdiction: 14 principles on the effective exercise of universal jurisdiction* (AI Index: IOR 53/01/99).

28 AI has prepared a *Checklist for Effective Implementation* (AI Index: IOR 40/11/00), which spells out what steps states should take to implement the Rome Statute of the International Criminal Court effectively.

29 *Torture in Russia – This man-made Hell* (AI Index EUR 46/04/97).

30 The members of CINAT are: Amnesty International; Association for the Prevention of Torture (APT); International Federation of Action of Christians for the Abolition of Torture (FIACAT); International Rehabilitation Council for Torture Victims (IRCT); Redress: Seeking Reparation for Torture Survivors; and World Organization Against Torture (OMCT).

31 For information aimed at NGOs on how to access the UN mechanisms, see: *The Torture Reporting Handbook: How to document and respond to allegations of torture within the international system for the protection of human rights,* Camille Giffard, Human Rights Centre, University of Essex, 2000. Available from the Human Rights Centre, University of Essex, Wivenhoe Park, Colchester CO4 3SQ, UK; http://www.essex.ac.uk/torturehandbook

32 *The Independent,* 25 May 2000

33 International Rehabilitation Council for Torture Victims (IRCT) website: http://www.irct.org/about_torture.htm

34 UN Doc CAT/C/16/D/41/1996.

35 Gorlick, Brian, "The Convention and the Committee against Torture: A Complementary Protection Regime for Refugees", in *International Journal of Refugee Law,* Vol.11, No.3, 1999.

36 Available in full at the Physicians for Human Rights website: http://www.phrusa.org/research/istanbul.html

37 UN Commission on Human Rights, resolution 2000/43, adopted 20 April 2000 (annex).

38 Minutes of the General Council of the Colegio Médico de Chile, 1 November 1985, cited in

Medicine Betrayed, British Medical Association, Zed Books, 1992.

39 In AI's view, the death penalty is the ultimate cruel, inhuman and degrading punishment. Because of the suffering involved in the execution itself and the harrowing experience of having to contemplate day after day one's intended death at the hands of the state, AI considers that it violates the right to be free from torture or other cruel or inhuman, degrading treatment or punishment, as well as the right to life.

40 "Helen versus hell", by Neil Belton, *The Guardian*, 10 January 1999.

41 *Captured Voices*, Victor Gollancz, London, 1999.

TAKE A STEP TO STAMP OUT TORTURE